# The Best Of Vanessa-Ann's Cross-Stitch Collection

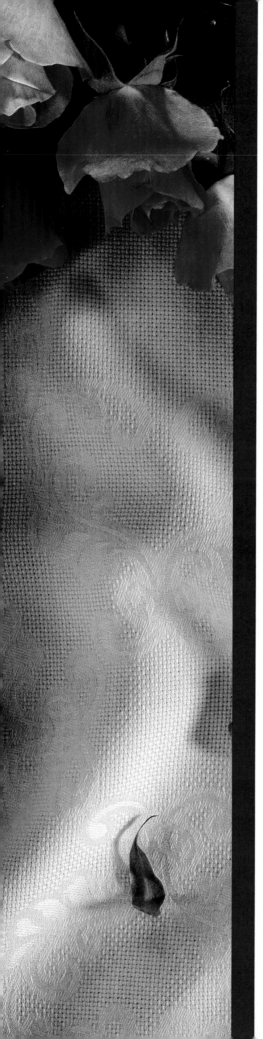

# The Vanessa-Ann Collection

### Owners
Jo Packham and Terrece Beesley

### Staff
Gloria Zirkel Baur

Sandra D. Chapman

Susan Jorgensen

Margaret Shields Marti

Barbara Milburn

Lisa Miles

Pamela Randall

Lynda Sessions Sorenson

Florence Stacey

Nancy Whitley

### Designers
Terrece Beesley

Trice Boerens

Linda Durbano

Tina Richards

### Book Design
Baker Design Group

### Photographer
Ryne Hazen

# The Best Of Vanessa-Ann's Cross-Stitch Collection

*Dedicated to the memory of my father, Charles Beesley (1913-1975).*

©1992 by Oxmoor House, Inc.
Book Division of Southern Progress Corporation
P.O. Box 2463, Birmingham, AL 35201

Library of Congress Catalog Number: 92-80928
ISBN: 0-8487-1112-2
Manufactured in the United States of America

First Printing

Editor-in-Chief: Nancy J. Fitzpatrick
Senior Editor, Editorial Services: Olivia Wells
Director of Manufacturing: Jerry Higdon
Art Director: James Boone

***The Best of Vanessa-Ann's Cross-Stitch Collection***
from the *Joys of Cross-Stitch* Series

Editor: Laurie Pate Sewell
Editorial Assistant: Shannon Leigh Sexton
Copy Chief: Mary Jean Haddin
Assistant Copy Editor: Susan Smith Cheatham
Production Manager: Rick Litton
Associate Production Manager: Theresa L. Beste
Production Assistant: Pam Beasley Bullock
Designer and Computer Artist: Larry Hunter

The Vanessa-Ann Collection extends its thanks to Trice Boerens, Diana Dunkley,
Penelope Hammons, Nick Kotok, Susan Pendleton, Nan Smith; Kaylene Interiors, Inc.;
Mary Gaskill's Trends and Traditions; The Treasure Basket, Ogden, Utah; The
Bearlace Cottage, Park City, Utah; Brigham Street Inn, Salt Lake City, Utah; and R.C.
Willey Home Furnishings, Syracuse, Utah.
Their trust and cooperation is gratefully acknowledged.

# Contents

## The Early Years

## From the Heart

## Everyday Pleasures

## Capture the Holiday Spirit

## New Creations

# The Early Years

*During the early years, Vanessa-Ann designs were available only in small pamphlets, and until now many of those designs were no longer in print. Here we proudly present some of the best works recaptured just for you in one exciting chapter. A bridal cornucopia filled with an elegant dried floral arrangement will be the perfect wedding keepsake. Trick-or-treat in style with our Halloween brew tote bag. Show a special friend how much you care with a sweet saying surrounded by a vividly stitched rainbow. And, for that precious little baby girl or boy, stitch a birth sampler to record important information.*

# Homeward Hearts

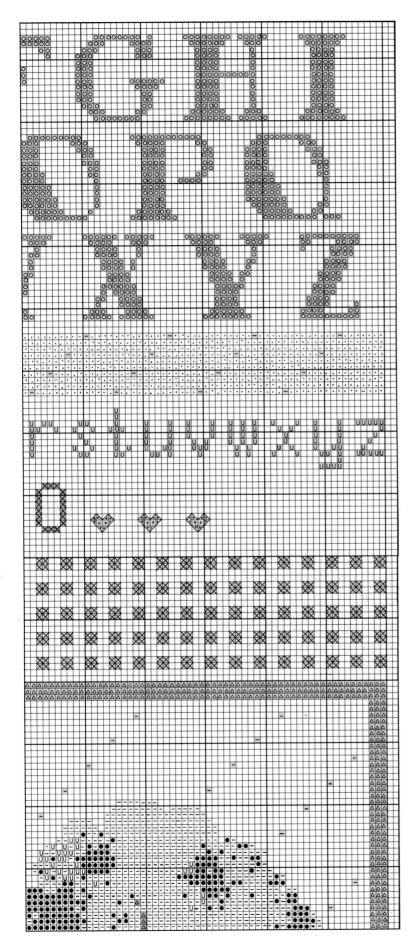

**SAMPLE**

Stitched on white Belfast Linen 32 over 2 threads, the finished design size is 10⅝" x 17⅛". The fabric was cut 17" x 24".

| FABRICS | DESIGN SIZES |
|---|---|
| Aida 11 | 15½" x 25⅛" |
| Aida 14 | 12⅛" x 19¾" |
| Aida 18 | 9½" x 15⅜" |
| Hardanger 22 | 7¾" x 12½" |

| Anchor | | DMC (used for sample) | |
|---|---|---|---|
| | | **Step 1: Cross-stitch (2 strands)** | |
| 1 | | White | |
| 386 | | 746 | Off White |
| 300 | | 745 | Yellow-lt. pale |
| 297 | | 743 | Yellow-med. |
| 303 | | 742 | Tangerine-lt. |
| 9 | | 760 | Salmon |
| 11 | | 3328 | Salmon-dk. |
| 13 | | 347 | Salmon-vy. dk. |
| 47 | | 321 | Christmas Red |
| 43 | | 815 | Garnet-med. |
| 44 | | 814 | Garnet-dk. |
| 159 | | 3325 | Baby Blue-lt. |
| 145 | | 334 | Baby Blue-med. |
| 978 | | 322 | Navy Blue-vy. lt. |
| 147 | | 312 | Navy Blue-lt. |
| 213 | | 369 | Pistachio Green-vy. lt. |
| 214 | | 368 | Pistachio Green-lt. |
| 215 | | 320 | Pistachio Green-med. |
| 246 | | 319 | Pistachio Green-vy. dk. |
| 265 | | 3348 | Yellow Green-lt. |
| 257 | | 3346 | Hunter Green |
| 227 | | 701 | Christmas Green-lt. |
| 370 | | 434 | Brown-lt. |
| 349 | | 301 | Mahogany-med. |
| 351 | | 400 | Mahogany-dk. |
| 378 | | 841 | Beige Brown-lt. |
| 379 | | 840 | Beige Brown-med. |
| 357 | | 801 | Coffee Brown-dk. |
| 905 | | 3031 | Mocha Brown-vy. dk. |
| 397 | | 762 | Pearl Gray-vy. lt. |
| 400 | | 414 | Steel Gray-dk. |
| 401 | | 317 | Pewter Gray |
| | | **Step 2: Backstitch (1 strand)** | |
| 382 | | 3371 | Black Brown |

**Stitch Count: 170 x 276**

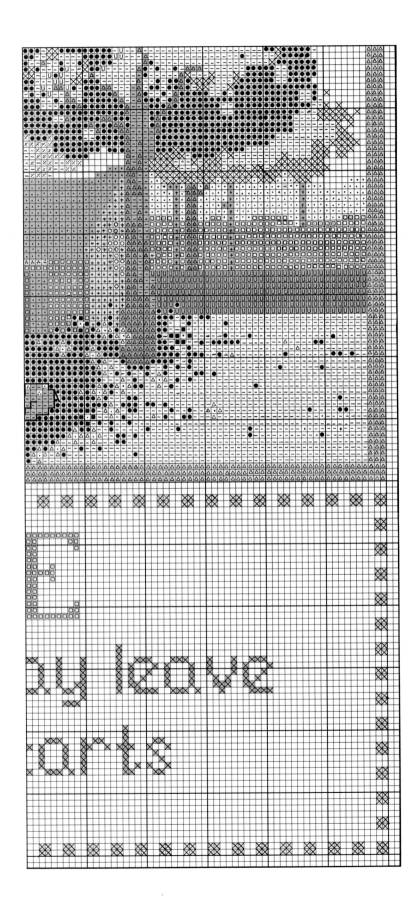

# Rainbow's End

| Anchor | | DMC | (used for sample) |
|---|---|---|---|

**Step 1:** Cross-stitch (2 strands)

| 289 | · | 307 | Lemon |
| 330 | – | 947 | Burnt Orange |
| 24 | △ | 776 | Pink-med. |
| 47 | ○ | 321 | Christmas Red |
| 104 | ◉ | 210 | Lavender-med. |
| 101 | ⊠ | 550 | Violet-vy. dk. |
| 132 | ✕ | 797 | Royal Blue |
| 239 | □ | 702 | Kelly Green |
| 879 | ▲ | 890 | Pistachio Green-ultra dk. |
| 403 | ■ | 310 | Black |

**Step 2:** Backstitch (1 strand)

| 403 | | 310 | Black |

**Step 3:** French Knot (1 strand)

| 403 | ● | 310 | Black |

**Stitch Count: 74 x 81**

**SAMPLE**

Stitched on white Aida 14 over 1 thread, the finished design size is 5¼" x 5¾". The fabric was cut 12" x 12".

**FABRICS**

Aida 11
Aida 18
Hardanger 22

**DESIGN SIZES**

6¾" x 7⅜"
4⅛" x 4½"
3⅜" x 3⅝"

# *Birth Announcements*

**SAMPLE**

Stitched on white Aida 18 over 1 thread, the finished design size for each is 8" x 10⅜". The fabric was cut 14" x 17". To personalize the sampler, transfer the letters and the numerals to graph paper. Mark the center of the graph and begin stitching in the center of the space indicated for personalizing.

| FABRICS | DESIGN SIZES |
|---|---|
| Aida 11 | 13⅛" x 16⅞" |
| Aida 14 | 10¼" x 13¼" |
| Hardanger 22 | 6½" x 8½" |

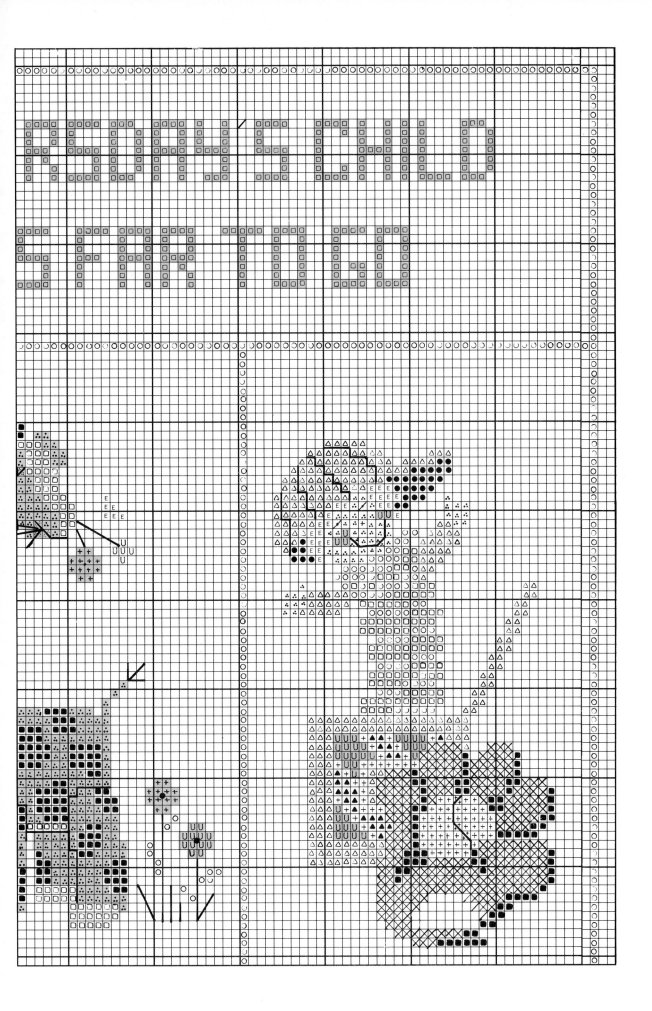

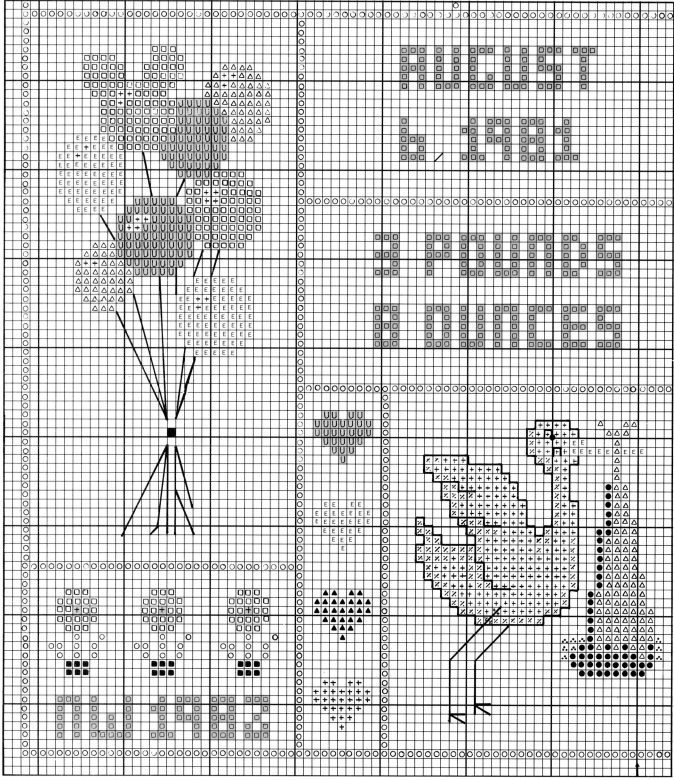

**Stitch Count: 144 x 186 (Boy Announcement)**

| Anchor | DMC (used for sample) | | |
|---|---|---|---|
| | **Step 1:** Cross-stitch (2 strands) | | |
| 1 | + | White | |
| 297 | □ | 743 | Yellow-med. |
| 4146 | ∴ | 754 | Peach-lt. |
| 333 | E | 608 | Orange Red |
| 335 | + | 606 | Orange Red-bright |
| 76 | U ∕ | 603 | Cranberry |
| 98 | ▲ | 553 | Violet-med. |

| | | | |
|---|---|---|---|
| 160 | △ | 813 | Blue-lt. |
| 162 | ● | 825 | Blue-dk. |
| 239 | ○ | 702 | Kelly Green |
| 307 | ∴ | 977 | Golden Brown-lt. |
| 308 | M | 976 | Golden Brown-med. |
| 308 | □ | 976 | Golden Brown-med. |
| 349 | ✕ | 301 | Mahogany-med. |
| 352 | ■ | 300 | Mahogany-vy. dk. |

| | | | |
|---|---|---|---|
| 382 | ∕ | 3371 | Black Brown |
| 398 | ✕ | 415 | Pearl Gray |
| | **Step 2:** Backstitch (1 strand) | | |
| 333 | ▬ | 608 | Orange Red (duck bills, stork legs, white edges of "C") |
| 76 | ▬ | 603 | Cranberry (mouth on jack-in-the-box) |
| 160 | ▬ | 813 | Blue-lt. (white edges of rattle) |

18

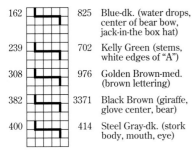

| 162 | | 825 | Blue-dk. (water drops, center of bear bow, jack-in-the box hat) |
| 239 | | 702 | Kelly Green (stems, white edges of "A") |
| 308 | | 976 | Golden Brown-med. (brown lettering) |
| 382 | | 3371 | Black Brown (giraffe, glove center, bear) |
| 400 | | 414 | Steel Gray-dk. (stork body, mouth, eye) |

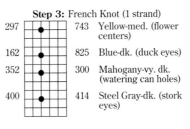

**Step 3:** French Knot (1 strand)

| 297 | ● | 743 | Yellow-med. (flower centers) |
| 162 | ● | 825 | Blue-dk. (duck eyes) |
| 352 | ● | 300 | Mahogany-vy. dk. (watering can holes) |
| 400 | ● | 414 | Steel Gray-dk. (stork eyes) |

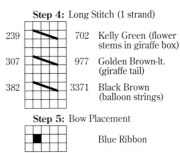

**Step 4:** Long Stitch (1 strand)

| 239 | ╱ | 702 | Kelly Green (flower stems in giraffe box) |
| 307 | ╱ | 977 | Golden Brown-lt. (giraffe tail) |
| 382 | ╱ | 3371 | Black Brown (balloon strings) |

**Step 5:** Bow Placement

■ Blue Ribbon

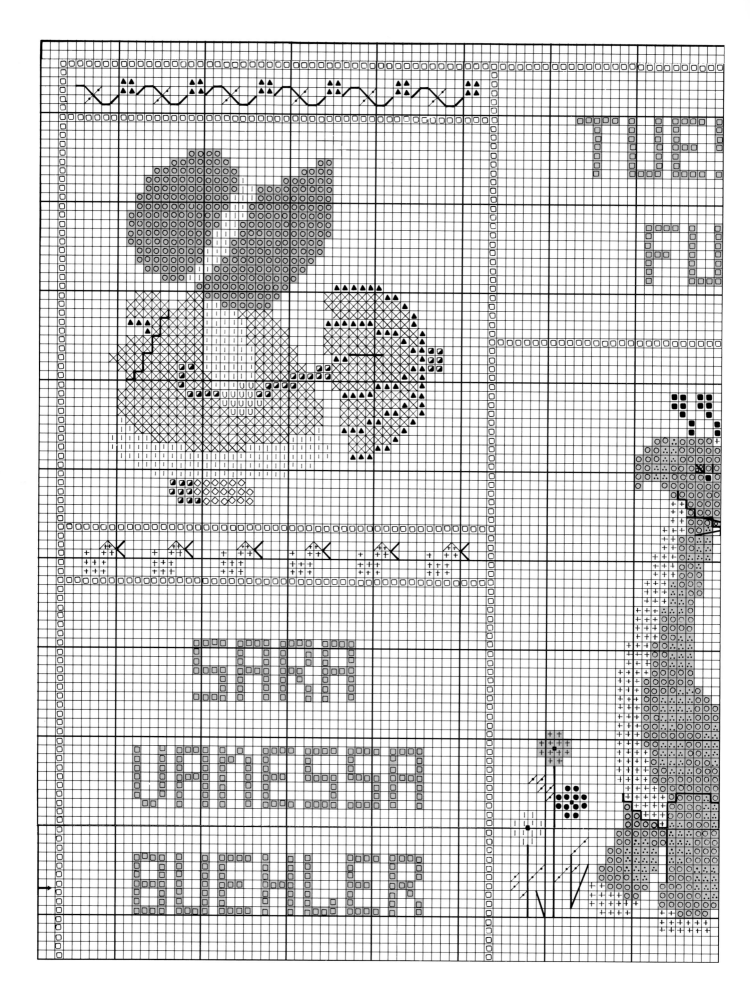

**Stitch Count 144 x 186 (Girl Announcement)**

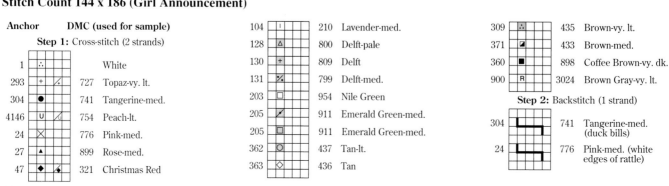

| Anchor | | DMC (used for sample) | | | | | | |
|---|---|---|---|---|---|---|---|---|
| **Step 1:** Cross-stitch (2 strands) | | | 104 | I | 210 | Lavender-med. | | |
| | | | 128 | △ | 800 | Delft-pale | | |
| 1 | ∴ | White | 130 | + | 809 | Delft | | |
| 293 | + / | 727 | Topaz-vy. lt. | 131 | ⊘ | 799 | Delft-med. |
| 304 | ● | 741 | Tangerine-med. | 203 | □ | 954 | Nile Green |
| 4146 | U / | 754 | Peach-lt. | 205 | / | 911 | Emerald Green-med. |
| 24 | X | 776 | Pink-med. | 205 | ▣ | 911 | Emerald Green-med. |
| 27 | ▲ | 899 | Rose-med. | 362 | ○ | 437 | Tan-lt. |
| 47 | ◆ / | 321 | Christmas Red | 363 | ◇ | 436 | Tan |

| Anchor | | DMC | |
|---|---|---|---|
| 309 | ∴ | 435 | Brown-vy. lt. |
| 371 | ◪ | 433 | Brown-med. |
| 360 | ■ | 898 | Coffee Brown-vy. dk. |
| 900 | R | 3024 | Brown Gray-vy. lt. |

**Step 2:** Backstitch (1 strand)

| 304 | ▬ | 741 | Tangerine-med. (duck bills) |
|---|---|---|---|
| 24 | ▬ | 776 | Pink-med. (white edges of rattle) |

| | | | |
|---|---|---|---|
| 27 | | 899 | Rose-med. (dress, heart in rainbow) |
| 104 | | 210 | Lavender-med. (white edges of "A") |
| 128 | | 800 | Delft-pale (white edges of "C") |
| 131 | | 799 | Delft-med. (center of bear bow) |
| 205 | | 911 | Emerald Green-med. (stems, lettering) |
| 362 | | 437 | Tan-lt. (giraffe's tail) |

| | | | |
|---|---|---|---|
| 371 | | 433 | Brown-med. (giraffe) |
| 357 | | 801 | Coffee Brown-dk. (bear) |
| 360 | | 898 | Coffee Brown-vy. dk. (house) |
| 900 | | 3024 | Brown Gray-vy. lt. (fence) |

**Step 3:** French Knot (1 strand)

| | | | |
|---|---|---|---|
| 360 | ■ | 898 | Coffee Brown-vy. dk. |

**Step 4:** Long Stitch (1 strand)

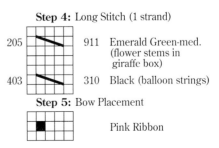

| | | | |
|---|---|---|---|
| 205 | | 911 | Emerald Green-med. (flower stems in giraffe box) |
| 403 | | 310 | Black (balloon strings) |

**Step 5:** Bow Placement

| | |
|---|---|
| | Pink Ribbon |

Monday's Child is fair of face.

Tuesday's child is full of grace.

Wednesday's child is full of woe.

Thursday's child has far to go.

Friday's child works hard for a living.

Saturday's child is loving and giving.

And the child that's born on the Sabbath day

Is bonny and blythe in every way.

# Something's Brewing

**SAMPLE**
Stitched on white Aida 14 over 1 thread, the finished design size is
9⅞" x 10⅛". The fabric was cut 16" x 17".

| FABRICS | DESIGN SIZES |
|---|---|
| Aida 11 | 12½" x 12⅞" |
| Aida 18 | 7⅝" x 7⅞" |
| Hardanger 22 | 6¼" x 6½" |

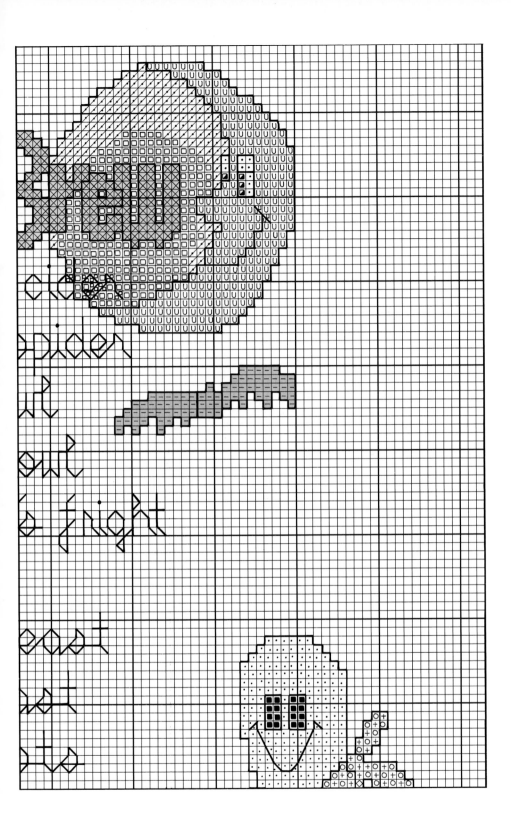

**Stitch Count: 138 x 142**

## MATERIALS

Completed cross-stitch design on white Aida 14; matching thread
½ yard of unstitched white Aida 14
½ yard of Halloween print fabric; matching thread
½ yard of polyester fleece

## DIRECTIONS

All seam allowances are ¼".

**1.** For bag front, with design centered, trim Aida to a 14½" square. From unstitched Aida, cut 1 (14½") square for back and 2 (3½" x 19") pieces for handles. From print fabric, cut 2 (14½") squares for lining. From fleece, cut 2 (14½") squares.

**2.** Baste 1 fleece square each to wrong side of bag front and back. With right sides facing and raw edges aligned, stitch bag front and back together around side and bottom edges, leaving top edge open. Trim batting from seam.

**3.** To make a boxed bottom, at 1 bottom corner of bag, align side and bottom seams by flattening bag, with right sides facing and with 1 seam on top of the other; finger-press seam allowances open. Stitch across corner as shown in Diagram. Repeat for other bottom corner. Clip corners and turn.

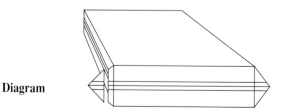

**Diagram**

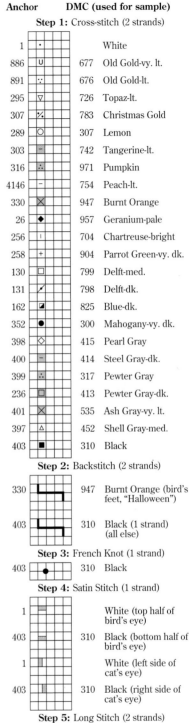

| Anchor | | DMC | (used for sample) |
|---|---|---|---|
| **Step 1: Cross-stitch (2 strands)** | | | |
| 1 | · | | White |
| 886 | U | 677 | Old Gold-vy. lt. |
| 891 | ∴ | 676 | Old Gold-lt. |
| 295 | ▽ | 726 | Topaz-lt. |
| 307 | ╱ | 783 | Christmas Gold |
| 289 | O | 307 | Lemon |
| 303 | ∷ | 742 | Tangerine-lt. |
| 316 | ∷ | 971 | Pumpkin |
| 4146 | – | 754 | Peach-lt. |
| 330 | ⊠ | 947 | Burnt Orange |
| 26 | ◆ | 957 | Geranium-pale |
| 256 | I | 704 | Chartreuse-bright |
| 258 | + | 904 | Parrot Green-vy. dk. |
| 130 | □ | 799 | Delft-med. |
| 131 | ╱ | 798 | Delft-dk. |
| 162 | ◪ | 825 | Blue-dk. |
| 352 | ● | 300 | Mahogany-vy. dk. |
| 398 | ◇ | 415 | Pearl Gray |
| 400 | – | 414 | Steel Gray-dk. |
| 399 | ∷ | 317 | Pewter Gray |
| 236 | ▣ | 413 | Pewter Gray-dk. |
| 401 | ⊠ | 535 | Ash Gray-vy. lt. |
| 397 | △ | 452 | Shell Gray-med. |
| 403 | ■ | 310 | Black |
| **Step 2: Backstitch (2 strands)** | | | |
| 330 | | 947 | Burnt Orange (bird's feet, "Halloween") |
| 403 | | 310 | Black (1 strand) (all else) |
| **Step 3: French Knot (1 strand)** | | | |
| 403 | ● | 310 | Black |
| **Step 4: Satin Stitch (1 strand)** | | | |
| 1 | | | White (top half of bird's eye) |
| 403 | | 310 | Black (bottom half of bird's eye) |
| 1 | | | White (left side of cat's eye) |
| 403 | | 310 | Black (right side of cat's eye) |
| **Step 5: Long Stitch (2 strands)** | | | |
| 403 | | 310 | Black (cat's whiskers) |

**4.** For lining, with right sides facing and raw edges aligned, stitch printed pieces together around side and bottom edges, leaving an opening in side seam. Referring to step 3 above, make boxed bottom. Do not turn lining.

**5.** To make handles, fold 1 (3½" x 19") piece in half lengthwise. Stitch long edges together. Turn. Press with seam centered. With right sides facing and raw edges aligned, pin each end of handle 3" from each side seam to top edge of bag front. Baste ends in place. Repeat with remaining handle on bag back. With right sides facing and seams aligned, slip lining over bag. Stitch around top edge, catching handles in seam. Turn through opening in lining. Tuck lining inside bag.

# A Gift from the Heart

| Anchor | | DMC (used for sample) | |
|---|---|---|---|
| | | **Step 1:** Cross-stitch (2 strands) | |
| 893 | ⊙ | 224 | Shell Pink-lt. |
| 970 | ▨ | 315 | Antique Mauve-vy. dk. |
| 871 | − | 3041 | Antique Violet-med. |
| 121 | ⊙ | 794 | Cornflower Blue-lt. |
| 928 | | 598 | Turquoise-lt. |
| 876 | ✕ | 502 | Blue Green |
| 832 | △ | 612 | Drab Brown-med. |
| 889 | ▲ | 610 | Drab Brown-vy. dk. |
| 401 | ▢ | 535 | Ash Gray-vy. lt. |
| 399 | + | 318 | Steel Gray-lt. |
| 403 | ● | 310 | Black |
| | | **Step 2:** Backstitch (1 strand) | |
| 401 | | 535 | Ash Gray-vy. lt. (girl in blue dress) |
| 403 | | 310 | Black (woman, girl in mauve dress) |
| | | **Step 3:** Long Stitch (1 strand) | |
| 401 | | 535 | Ash Gray-vy. lt. (strings) |

**Stitch Count: 85 x 86**

## SAMPLE

Stitched on white Linda 27 over 2 threads, the finished design size is 6¼" x 6⅜". The fabric was cut 12" x 12".

| FABRICS | DESIGN SIZES |
|---|---|
| Aida 11 | 7¾" x 7⅞" |
| Aida 14 | 6⅛" x 6⅛" |
| Aida 18 | 4¾" x 4¾" |
| Hardanger 22 | 3⅞" x 3⅞" |

# Folk Sampler

## SAMPLE

Stitched on beige Hardanger 22 over 1 and 2 threads, the finished design size is 15⅜" x 26⅜". The fabric was cut 22" x 33". Use 1 strand of embroidery floss when stitching over 1 thread and 2 strands when stitching over 2 threads. Note that sections stitched over 1 thread have a smaller grid than those stitched over 2 threads.  To accommodate the 2 sizes of stitches, this design must be stitched on monoweave fabric. To personalize the sampler, transfer letters and numerals to graph paper. Mark center of graph and begin stitching in center of space indicated for personalizing.

| FABRICS | DESIGN SIZES |
|---|---|
| Linda 27 | 12½" x 21½" |
| Murano 30 | 11¼" x 19⅜" |
| Belfast Linen 32 | 10½" x 18⅛" |

34

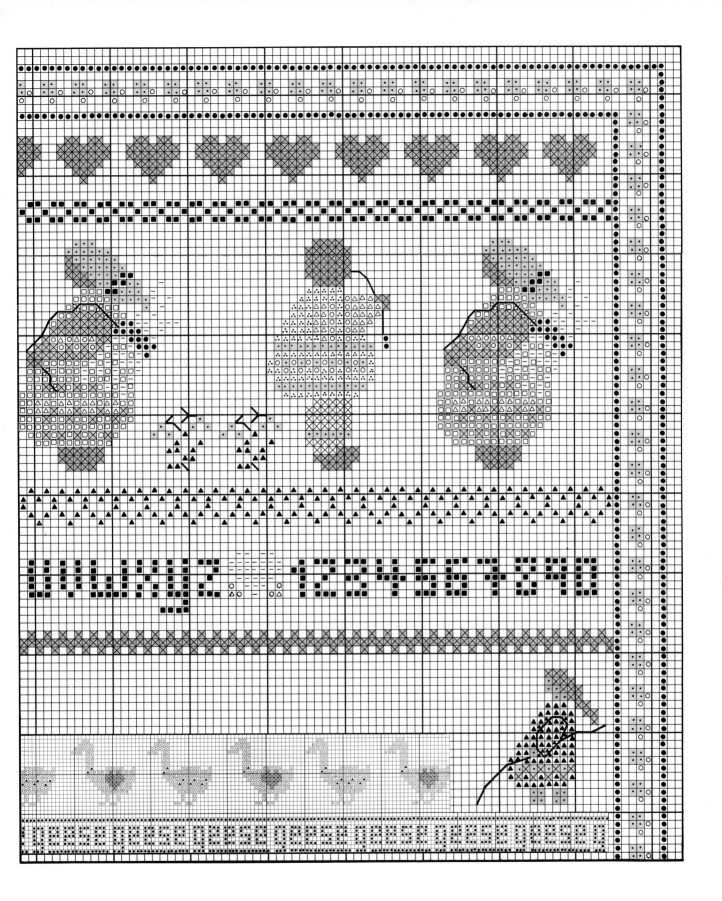

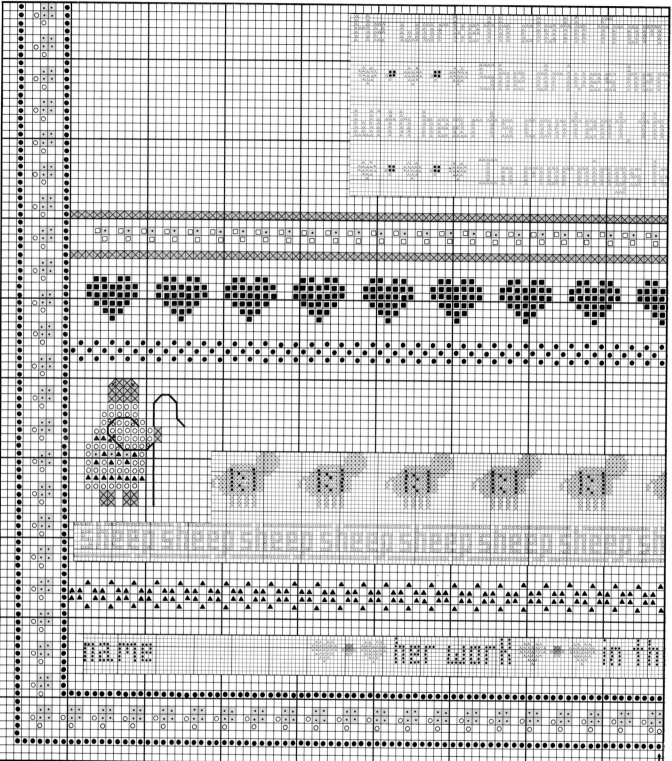

**Stitch Count: 169 x 290**

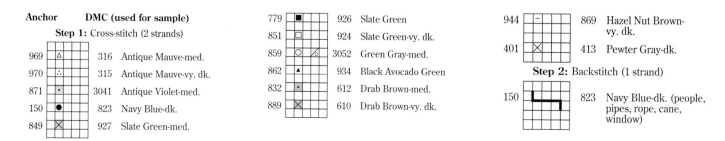

Anchor  DMC (used for sample)

**Step 1:** Cross-stitch (2 strands)

| Anchor | | DMC | |
|---|---|---|---|
| 969 | △ | 316 | Antique Mauve-med. |
| 970 | ∴ | 315 | Antique Mauve-vy. dk. |
| 871 | · | 3041 | Antique Violet-med. |
| 150 | ● | 823 | Navy Blue-dk. |
| 849 | ✕ | 927 | Slate Green-med. |

| | | | |
|---|---|---|---|
| 779 | ■ | 926 | Slate Green |
| 851 | □ | 924 | Slate Green-vy. dk. |
| 859 | ○ / | 3052 | Green Gray-med. |
| 862 | ▲ | 934 | Black Avocado Green |
| 832 | | 612 | Drab Brown-med. |
| 889 | ✕ | 610 | Drab Brown-vy. dk. |

| | | | |
|---|---|---|---|
| 944 | − | 869 | Hazel Nut Brown-vy. dk. |
| 401 | ✕ | 413 | Pewter Gray-dk. |

**Step 2:** Backstitch (1 strand)

| | | | |
|---|---|---|---|
| 150 | ⌐ | 823 | Navy Blue-dk. (people, pipes, rope, cane, window) |

38

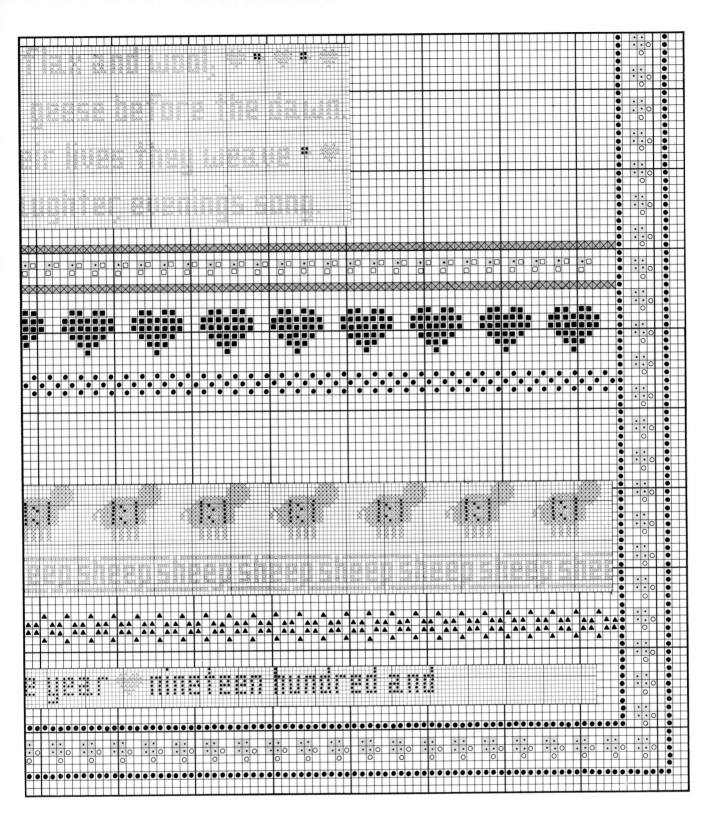

 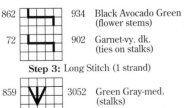

# Wedding Keepsake

**SAMPLE**

Stitched on white Belfast Linen 32 over 2 threads, the finished design size is 8" x 4⅜". The fabric was cut 15" x 15".

| FABRICS | DESIGN SIZES |
|---|---|
| Aida 11 | 11½" x 6⅜" |
| Aida 14 | 9⅛" x 5" |
| Aida 18 | 7" x 3⅞" |
| Hardanger 22 | 5¾" x 3⅛" |

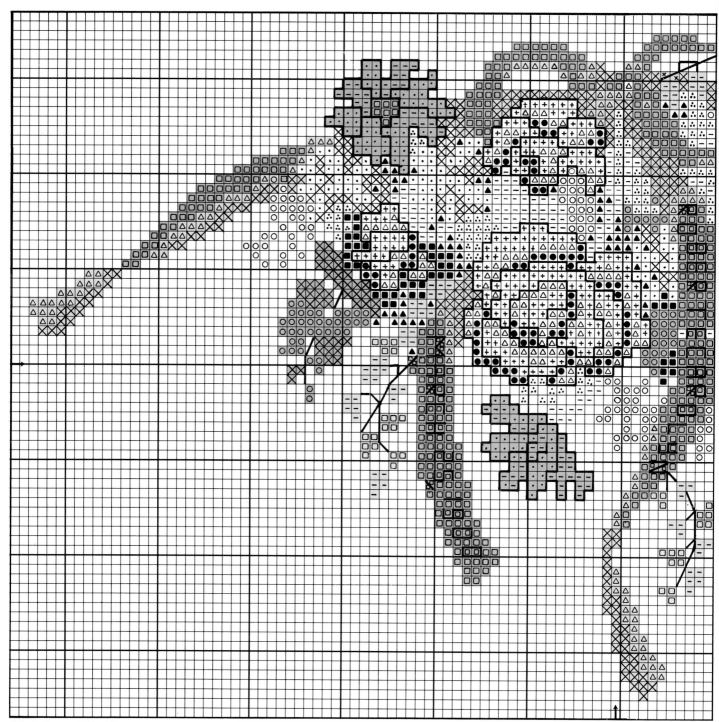

**Stitch Count: 127 x 70**

## MATERIALS
Completed design on white Belfast Linen 32; matching thread
15" square of white fabric for lining
2 (15") squares of heavy crinoline
¾ yard (¾"-wide) double-edged gold trim
Dried flower bouquet

## DIRECTIONS
All seam allowances are ¼".

**1.** Enlarge pattern. Place pattern on design piece with top edge of pattern 1½" above and parallel to top row of stitching. Cut out. From white fabric, cut 1 piece for lining. From crinoline, cut 2 pieces ¼" smaller all around than pattern.

**2.** With right sides facing, stitch design piece and lining together, leaving 1 straight edge open. Clip corners and turn. Handling crinoline pieces as 1, insert between design piece and lining, fitting carefully into corners. Turn under seam allowance and slipstitch opening closed.

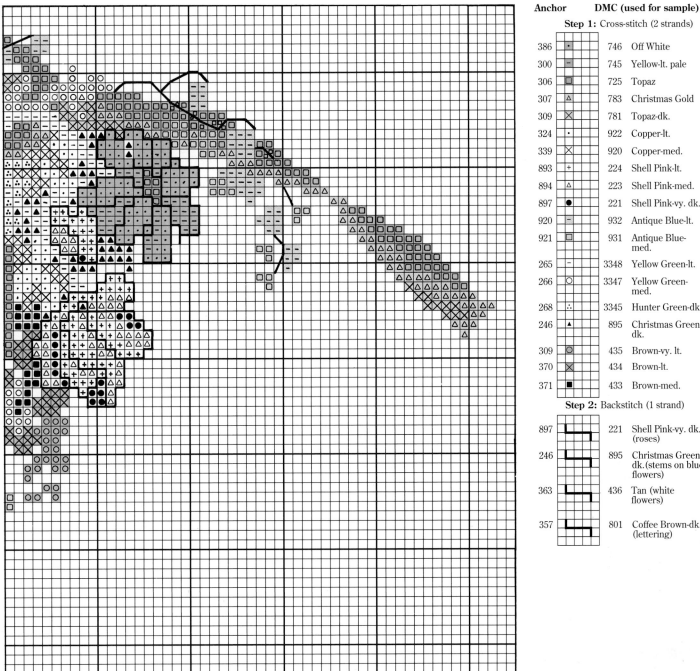

**3.** To form cornucopia, carefully roll design piece into a cone, overlapping straight edges ½". Slipstitch straight edges together.

**4.** Tack gold trim around top edge and down center back seam. Fill with dried flower bouquet.

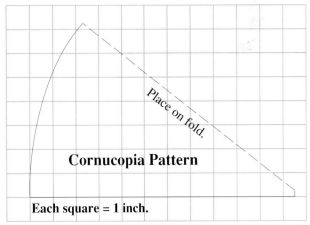

**Cornucopia Pattern**

Place on fold.

**Each square = 1 inch.**

# From The Heart

Sentiments can be expressed in many different ways—a friendly gesture, a kind word, or a special handmade gift. In this chapter, you'll find a collection of designs that will help convey your feelings. An elegant sampler showing the names and birthdates of those special grandchildren is sure to be a treasure for Grandma and Grandpa. A richly colored table runner will add warmth to the family's Thanksgiving dinner. Greet your friends with a floral wreath that spells out "Welcome," or stitch up an extra-special piece that says "I Love You" for someone dear.

# My Grandchildren

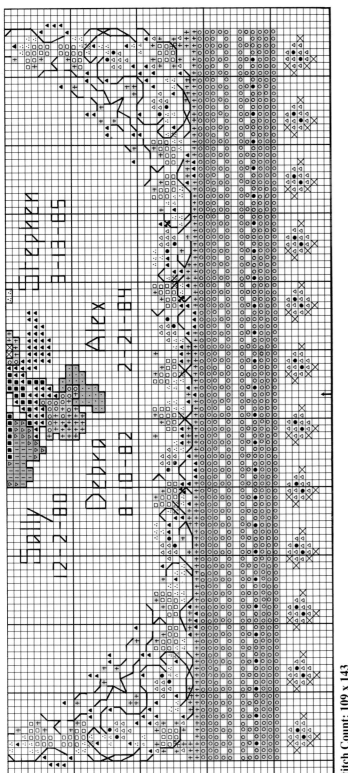

**Stitch Count: 109 x 143**

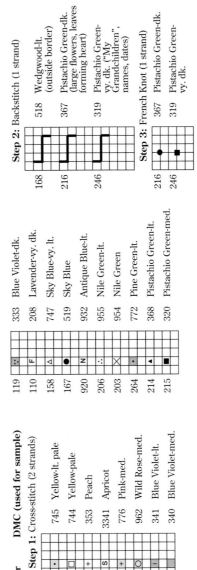

| Anchor | | DMC (used for sample) |
|---|---|---|
| **Step 1: Cross-stitch (2 strands)** | | |
| 300 | 745 | Yellow-lt. pale |
| 301 | 744 | Yellow-pale |
| 8 | 353 | Peach |
| 328 | 3341 | Apricot |
| 24 | 776 | Pink-med. |
| 76 | 962 | Wild Rose-med. |
| 117 | 341 | Blue Violet-lt. |
| 118 | 340 | Blue Violet-med. |
| 119 | 333 | Blue Violet-dk. |
| 110 | 208 | Lavender-vy. dk. |
| 158 | 747 | Sky Blue-vy. lt. |
| 167 | 519 | Sky Blue |
| 920 | 932 | Antique Blue-lt. |
| 206 | 955 | Nile Green-lt. |
| 203 | 954 | Nile Green |
| 264 | 772 | Pine Green-lt. |
| 214 | 368 | Pistachio Green-lt. |
| 215 | 320 | Pistachio Green-med. |
| **Step 2: Backstitch (1 strand)** | | |
| 168 | 518 | Wedgwood-lt. (outside border) |
| 216 | 367 | Pistachio Green-dk. (large flowers, leaves forming heart) |
| 246 | 319 | Pistachio Green-vy. dk. ("My Grandchildren", names, dates) |
| **Step 3: French Knot (1 strand)** | | |
| 216 | 367 | Pistachio Green-dk. |
| 246 | 319 | Pistachio Green-vy. dk. |

## SAMPLE

Stitched on cream Belfast Linen 32 over 2 threads, the finished design size is 6¾" x 9". The fabric was cut 13" x 15". To personalize the design, transfer names and dates of birth to graph paper, centering each date below corresponding name. Mark the center of the graph and begin stitching in the center of the space indicated.

| FABRICS | DESIGN SIZES |
|---|---|
| Aida 11 | 9⅞" x 13" |
| Aida 14 | 7¾" x 10¼" |
| Aida 18 | 6" x 8" |
| Hardanger 22 | 5" x 6½" |

# I Love You

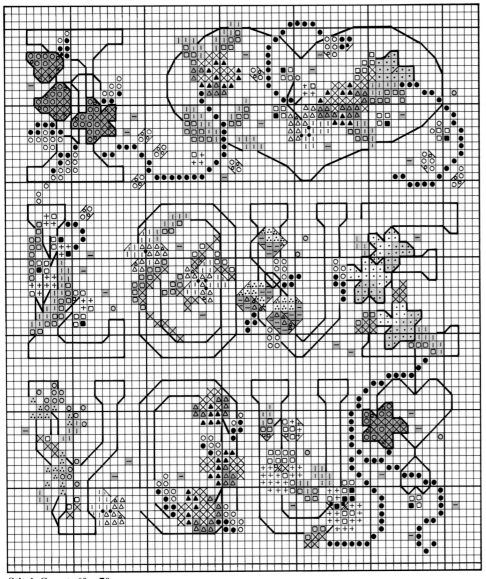

**Stitch Count: 60 x 70**

| Anchor | | | DMC | (used for sample) |
|---|---|---|---|---|
| **Step 1:** Cross-stitch (2 strands) | | | | |
| 1 | · | ⁄ | | White |
| 386 | ○ | ⁄ | 746 | Off White |
| 301 | ✕ | ⁄ | 744 | Yellow-pale |
| 328 | △ | ⁄ | 3341 | Apricot |
| 329 | I | ⁄ | 3340 | Apricot-med. |
| 25 | ∴ | ⁄ | 3326 | Rose-lt. |
| 27 | − | ⁄ | 899 | Rose-med. |
| 42 | △ · | ⁄ | 335 | Rose |
| 43 | ✕ | ⁄ | 3350 | Dusty Rose-dk. |
| 70 | ▲ | | 3685 | Mauve-dk. |
| 108 | + | ⁄ | 211 | Lavender-lt. |
| 110 | ■ | ⁄ | 208 | Lavender-vy. dk. |
| 95 | □ | ⁄ | 554 | Violet-lt. |
| 158 | · | ⁄ | 747 | Sky Blue-vy. lt. |
| 130 | ○ | | 799 | Delft-med. |
| 131 | ∴ | | 798 | Delft-dk. |
| 187 | ○ | ⁄ | 992 | Aquamarine |
| 189 | ● | ⁄ | 991 | Aquamarine-dk. |
| 208 | I | | 563 | Jade-lt. |
| 210 | □ | ⁄ | 562 | Jade-med. |
| 212 | ✕ | ⁄ | 561 | Jade-vy. dk. |
| **Step 2:** Backstitch (1 strand) | | | | |
| 304 | | | 741 | Tangerine-med. (yellow flowers) |
| 70 | | | 3685 | Mauve-dk. (lettering, hearts) |
| 130 | | | 799 | Delft-med. (blue flowers) |
| 189 | | | 991 | Aquamarine-dk. (stems) |
| **Step 3:** French Knot (1 strand) | | | | |
| 70 | ● | | 3685 | Mauve-dk. |

**SAMPLE**

Stitched on white Belfast Linen 32 over 2 threads, the finished design size is 3¾" x 4⅜". The fabric was cut 10" x 11".

| FABRICS | DESIGN SIZES |
|---|---|
| Aida 11 | 5½" x 6⅜" |
| Aida 14 | 4¼" x 5" |
| Aida 18 | 3⅛" x 3⅞" |
| Hardanger 22 | 2¾" x 3⅛" |

# Special Delivery Cupids

**Stitch Count: 94 x 70**

# SAMPLE

Stitched on white Belfast Linen 32 over 2 threads, the finished design size is 5⅞" x 4⅜". Fabric was cut 12" x 11".

| FABRICS | DESIGN SIZES |
|---------|--------------|
| Aida 11 | 8½" x 6⅜" |
| Aida 14 | 6¾" x 5" |
| Aida 18 | 5¼" x 3⅞" |
| Hardanger 22 | 4¼" x 3⅛" |

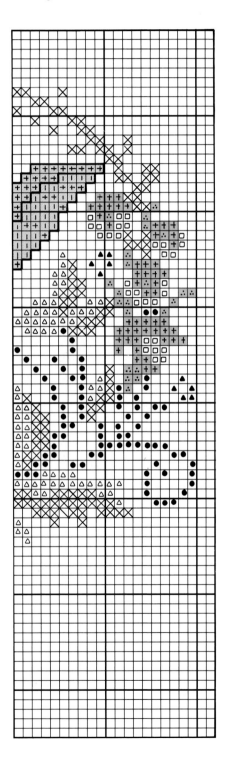

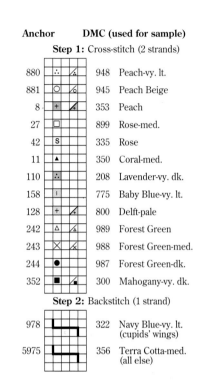

| Anchor | | DMC (used for sample) |
|--------|--|------------------------|
| **Step 1: Cross-stitch (2 strands)** | | |
| 880 | | 948 Peach-vy. lt. |
| 881 | | 945 Peach Beige |
| 8 | | 353 Peach |
| 27 | | 899 Rose-med. |
| 42 | | 335 Rose |
| 11 | | 350 Coral-med. |
| 110 | | 208 Lavender-vy. dk. |
| 158 | | 775 Baby Blue-vy. lt. |
| 128 | | 800 Delft-pale |
| 242 | | 989 Forest Green |
| 243 | | 988 Forest Green-med. |
| 244 | | 987 Forest Green-dk. |
| 352 | | 300 Mahogany-vy. dk. |
| **Step 2: Backstitch (1 strand)** | | |
| 978 | | 322 Navy Blue-vy. lt. (cupids' wings) |
| 5975 | | 356 Terra Cotta-med. (all else) |

# Bunny Bouquet

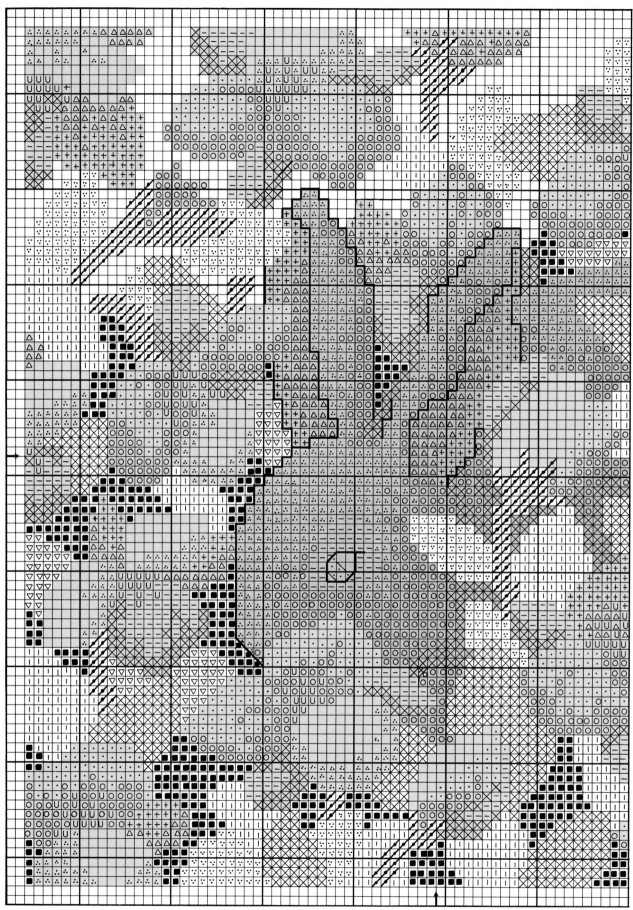

**Stitch Count: 90 x 90**

54

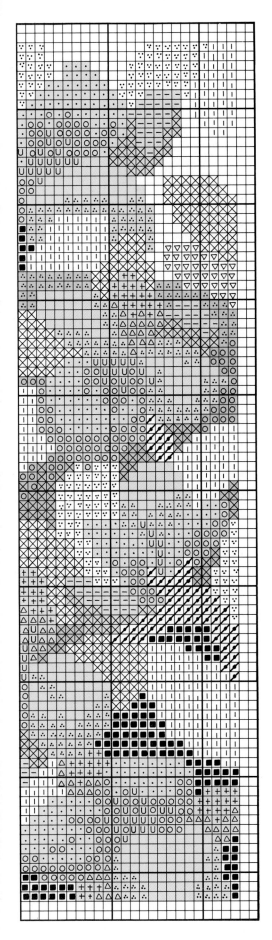

## SAMPLE

Stitched on Wedgwood Murano 30 over 2 threads, the finished design size is 6" x 6". The fabric was cut 12" x 12".

| FABRICS | DESIGN SIZES |
|---|---|
| Aida 11 | 8⅛" x 8⅛" |
| Aida 14 | 6⅜" x 6⅜" |
| Aida 18 | 5" x 5" |
| Hardanger 22 | 4⅛" x 4⅛" |

| Anchor | | DMC (used for sample) | |
|---|---|---|---|

**Step 1:** Cross-stitch (2 strands)

| Anchor | | DMC | |
|---|---|---|---|
| 303 | U | 742 | Tangerine-lt. |
| 26 | | 3708 | Melon-lt. |
| 28 | ∴ | 3706 | Melon-med. |
| 75 | • | 604 | Cranberry-lt. |
| 76 | O | 603 | Cranberry |
| 86 | − | 3608 | Plum-vy. lt. |
| 87 | X | 3607 | Plum-lt. |
| 95 | + | 554 | Violet-lt. |
| 98 | △ | 553 | Violet-med. |
| 186 | I | 993 | Aquamarine-lt. |
| 203 | ╱ | 954 | Nile Green |
| 204 | X | 912 | Emerald Green-lt. |
| 210 | ▽ | 562 | Jade-med. |
| 212 | ∴ | 561 | Jade-vy. dk. |
| 879 | ■ | 500 | Blue Green-vy. dk. |
| 885 | + | 739 | Tan-ultra vy. lt. |
| 942 | △ | 738 | Tan-vy. lt. |
| 4146 | − | 950 | Peach Pecan-dk. |
| 914 | ∴ | 3064 | Pecan-lt. |
| 914 | O | 3064 | Pecan-lt. (1 strand) + |
| 936 | | 632 | Pecan-dk. (1 strand) |
| 936 | X | 632 | Pecan-dk. |

**Step 2:** Satin Stitch (1 strand)

| Anchor | | DMC | |
|---|---|---|---|
| 8581 | • | 3022 | Brown Gray-med. |
| 382 | | 3021 | Brown Gray-vy. dk. |

**Step 3:** Backstitch (1 strand)

| Anchor | | DMC | |
|---|---|---|---|
| 936 | ⌐ | 632 | Pecan-dk. (bunny ears, head) |
| 382 | ⌐ | 3021 | Brown Gray-vy. dk. (around eye) |

# *Bountiful Harvest Table Runner*

## SAMPLE

Stitched on Vanessa-Ann Afghan Weave 18 over 1 thread. The fabric was cut 24" x 58" (the width measurement includes 3 whole blocks and ½ block on each side). The stitching area of each woven block is 88 x 88. The heavy black lines surrounding each graph indicate the block boundaries. (See Diagram for placement.) Stitch design on each end of runner. See Suppliers for Afghan material and Overture yarn.

## MATERIALS

Completed cross-stitch on Vanessa-Ann Afghan Weave 18; matching thread
Overture variegated yarn: 10 skeins Spices (color V58)
Size 4 steel crochet hook

## DIRECTIONS

**1.** To hem runner, turn under ½" twice along all raw edges, mitering corners. Slipstitch hem in place.

**2.** *Note:* See page 62 for crochet abbreviations. Separate yarn into 4 single strands. Work first row of crochet stitches under 2 or 3 threads of fabric at folded edge of hem. *Row 1:* With runner turned to work across 1 cross-stitched end, join 1 strand of yarn in corner, sc in same place, * ch 5, sk 13 or 14 threads, sc between next 2 threads, rep from * across, end with sc in corner = 30 sc and 29 ch-5 sps. Turn. *Row 2:* Sl st into ch-5 sp, ch 3 for first dc, 3 dc in same sp, * ch 3, 4 dc in next sp, rep from * across = 29 4-dc groups. Turn. *Row 3: Beginning half-triangle:* Ch 6 for first dc and ch 3, 4 dc in next sp, ch 3, 4 dc in next sp, turn, sl st into next ch-3 sp, ch 3 for dc, 3 dc in same sp, ch 3, 4 dc in next sp, turn, ch 6 for dc and ch 3, 4 dc in next sp. Fasten off. *Triangle:* Sk next 4-dc group on row 2, join yarn in next ch-3 sp, ch 3 for first dc, 3 dc in same sp, (ch 3, 4 dc in next sp) 7 times, turn, * sl st into next ch-3 sp, ch 3 for first dc, 3 dc in same sp, (ch 3, 4 dc in next sp) across, turn, rep from * 5 times more. Fasten off. Rep triangle as established twice more. *Ending half-triangle:* Sk next 4-dc group on Row 2, join yarn in next ch-3 sp, ch 3 for first dc, 3 dc in same sp, ch 3, 4 dc in next sp, ch 3, sk 3 dc, dc in next dc, turn, ch 3 for dc, 3 dc in sp, ch 3, 4 dc in next sp, turn, sl st into next ch-3 sp, ch 3 for dc, 3 dc in same sp, ch 3, sk 3 dc, dc in next dc. Fasten off. Repeat for remaining end of runner.

**3.** For each tassel, cut 5 (18") lengths of yarn (do not separate plies). Make 10 tassels. Knot a tassel in the ch-3 sp at the point of each triangle and half-triangle on each end of runner.

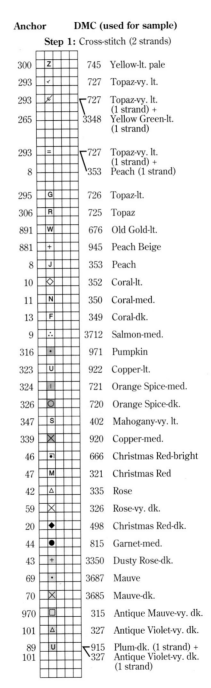

| Anchor | | DMC (used for sample) | |
|---|---|---|---|
| | | **Step 1: Cross-stitch (2 strands)** | |
| 300 | Z | 745 | Yellow-lt. pale |
| 293 | ˅ | 727 | Topaz-vy. lt. |
| 293 | ✍ | 727 | Topaz-vy. lt. (1 strand) + |
| 265 | | 3348 | Yellow Green-lt. (1 strand) |
| 293 | = | 727 | Topaz-vy. lt. (1 strand) + |
| 8 | | 353 | Peach (1 strand) |
| 295 | G | 726 | Topaz-lt. |
| 306 | R | 725 | Topaz |
| 891 | W | 676 | Old Gold-lt. |
| 881 | + | 945 | Peach Beige |
| 8 | J | 353 | Peach |
| 10 | ◇ | 352 | Coral-lt. |
| 11 | N | 350 | Coral-med. |
| 13 | F | 349 | Coral-dk. |
| 9 | ∴ | 3712 | Salmon-med. |
| 316 | • | 971 | Pumpkin |
| 323 | U | 922 | Copper-lt. |
| 324 | I | 721 | Orange Spice-med. |
| 326 | O | 720 | Orange Spice-dk. |
| 347 | S | 402 | Mahogany-vy. lt. |
| 339 | ✕ | 920 | Copper-med. |
| 46 | ◙ | 666 | Christmas Red-bright |
| 47 | M | 321 | Christmas Red |
| 42 | △ | 335 | Rose |
| 59 | ✕ | 326 | Rose-vy. dk. |
| 20 | ◆ | 498 | Christmas Red-dk. |
| 44 | ● | 815 | Garnet-med. |
| 43 | + | 3350 | Dusty Rose-dk. |
| 69 | · | 3687 | Mauve |
| 70 | ✕ | 3685 | Mauve-dk. |
| 970 | □ | 315 | Antique Mauve-vy. dk. |
| 101 | △ | 327 | Antique Violet-vy. dk. |
| 89 | U | 915 | Plum-dk. (1 strand) + |
| 101 | | 327 | Antique Violet-vy. dk. (1 strand) |

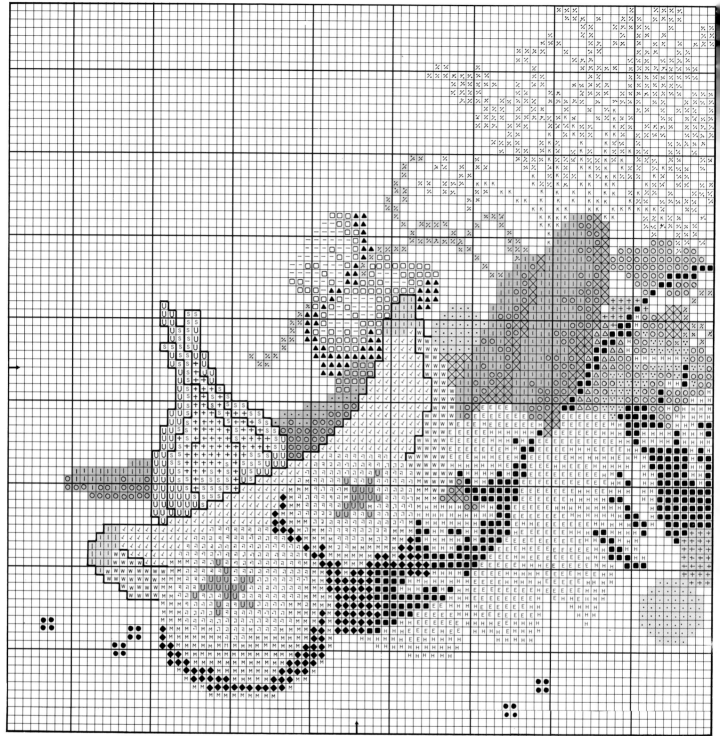

**Stitch Count: 84 x 86  (Section A)**

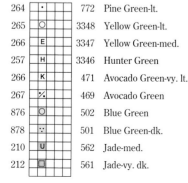
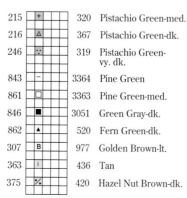

| | | | | |
|---|---|---|---|---|
| 264 | · | 772 | Pine Green-lt. |
| 265 | O | 3348 | Yellow Green-lt. |
| 266 | E | 3347 | Yellow Green-med. |
| 257 | H | 3346 | Hunter Green |
| 266 | K | 471 | Avocado Green-vy. lt. |
| 267 | ⅍ | 469 | Avocado Green |
| 876 | ⊙ | 502 | Blue Green |
| 878 | ∴ | 501 | Blue Green-dk. |
| 210 | U | 562 | Jade-med. |
| 212 | ▣ | 561 | Jade-vy. dk. |

| | | | | |
|---|---|---|---|---|
| 215 | + | 320 | Pistachio Green-med. |
| 216 | △ | 367 | Pistachio Green-dk. |
| 246 | ∷ | 319 | Pistachio Green-vy. dk. |
| 843 | − | 3364 | Pine Green |
| 861 | ☐ | 3363 | Pine Green-med. |
| 846 | ■ | 3051 | Green Gray-dk. |
| 862 | ▲ | 520 | Fern Green-dk. |
| 307 | B | 977 | Golden Brown-lt. |
| 363 | ı | 436 | Tan |
| 375 | ⅍ | 420 | Hazel Nut Brown-dk. |

**Step 2:** Backstitch (1 strand)

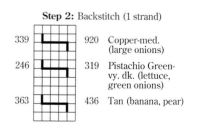

| | | | |
|---|---|---|---|
| 339 | | 920 | Copper-med. (large onions) |
| 246 | | 319 | Pistachio Green-vy. dk. (lettuce, green onions) |
| 363 | | 436 | Tan (banana, pear) |

58

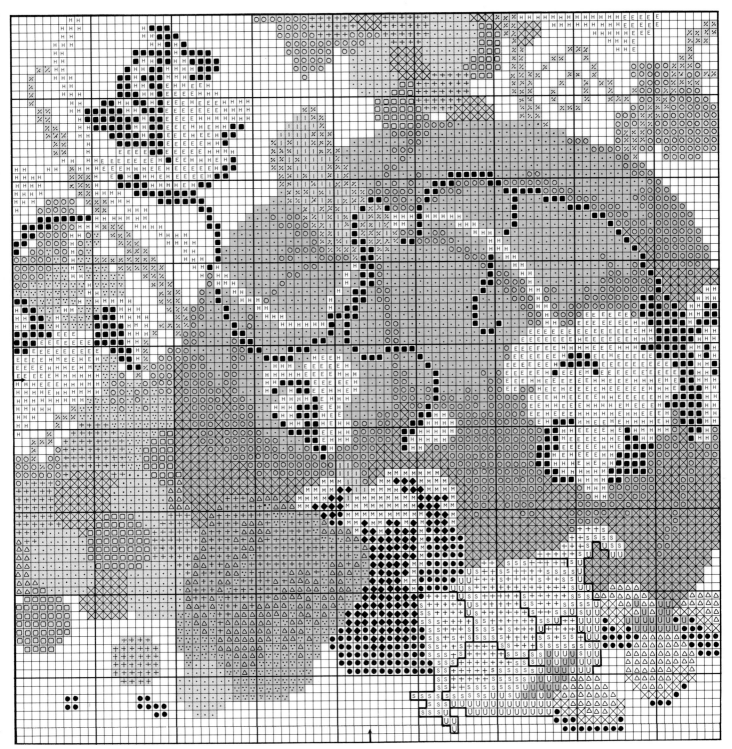

**Stitch Count: 88 x 87  (Section B)**

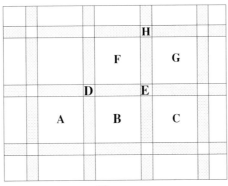

**Diagram**

**Stitch Count: 86 x 83 (Section C)**

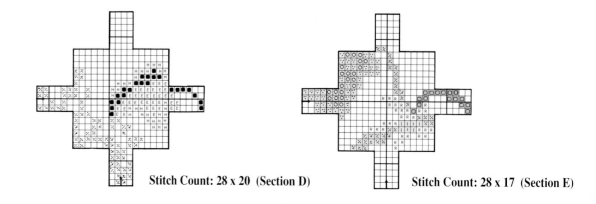

**Stitch Count: 28 x 20 (Section D)**

**Stitch Count: 28 x 17 (Section E)**

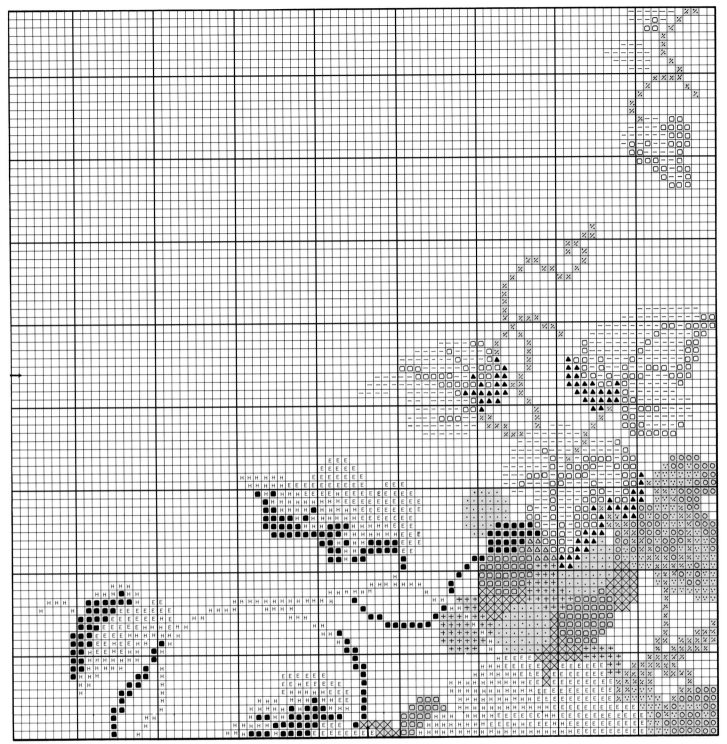

**Stitch Count: 85 x 88  (Section F)**

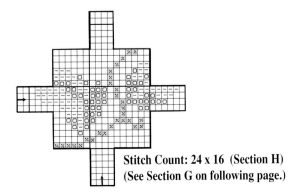

**Stitch Count: 24 x 16  (Section H)**
**(See Section G on following page.)**

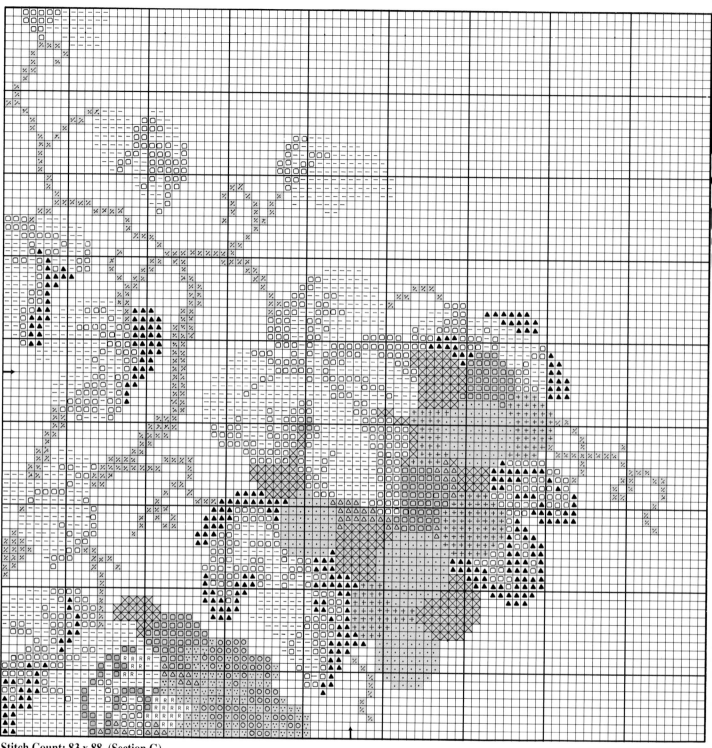

**Stitch Count: 83 x 88 (Section G)**

**CROCHET ABBREVIATIONS**

**ch**—chain

**dc**—double crochet

**rep**—repeat

**sc**—single crochet

**sk**—skip

**sl st**—slip stitch

**sp(s)**—space(s)

# Welcome Wreath

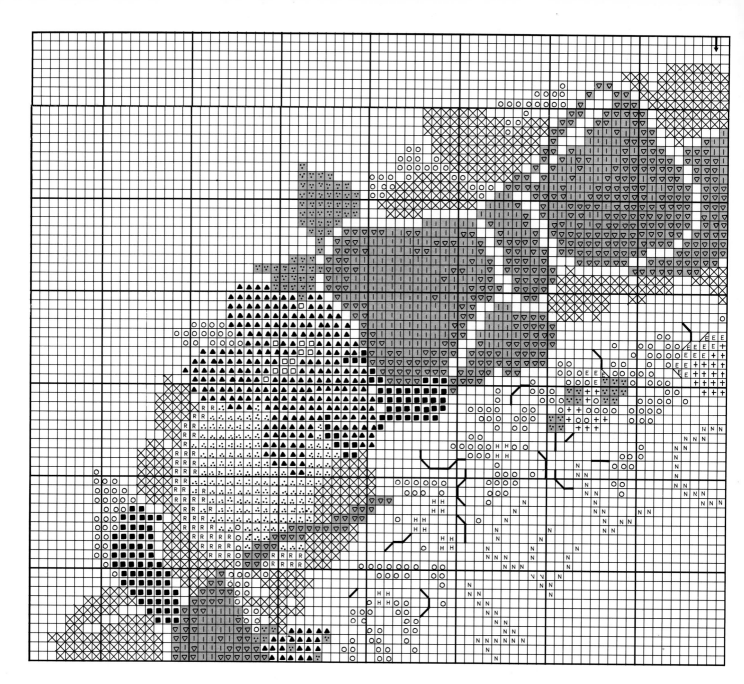

**SAMPLE**
Stitched on cream Belfast Linen 32 over 2 threads, the finished design size is 9¼" x 9¼". The fabric was cut 16" x 16".

| FABRICS | DESIGN SIZES |
|---|---|
| Aida 11 | 13½" x 13½" |
| Aida 14 | 10⅝" x 10⅝" |
| Aida 18 | 8¼" x 8¼" |
| Hardanger 22 | 6¾" x 6¾" |

**Stitch Count: 149 x 148**

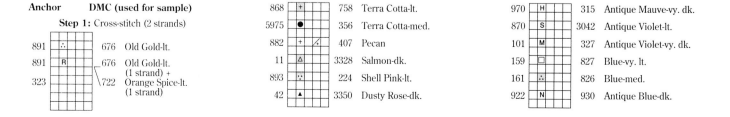

| Anchor | | DMC (used for sample) |
|---|---|---|
| **Step 1:** Cross-stitch (2 strands) | | |
| 891 | | 676 Old Gold-lt. |
| 891 | R | 676 Old Gold-lt. (1 strand) + |
| 323 | | 722 Orange Spice-lt. (1 strand) |

| | | |
|---|---|---|
| 868 | + | 758 Terra Cotta-lt. |
| 5975 | ● | 356 Terra Cotta-med. |
| 882 | + / | 407 Pecan |
| 11 | △ | 3328 Salmon-dk. |
| 893 | | 224 Shell Pink-lt. |
| 42 | ▲ | 3350 Dusty Rose-dk. |

| | | |
|---|---|---|
| 970 | H | 315 Antique Mauve-vy. dk. |
| 870 | S | 3042 Antique Violet-lt. |
| 101 | M | 327 Antique Violet-vy. dk. |
| 159 | □ | 827 Blue-vy. lt. |
| 161 | | 826 Blue-med. |
| 922 | N | 930 Antique Blue-dk. |

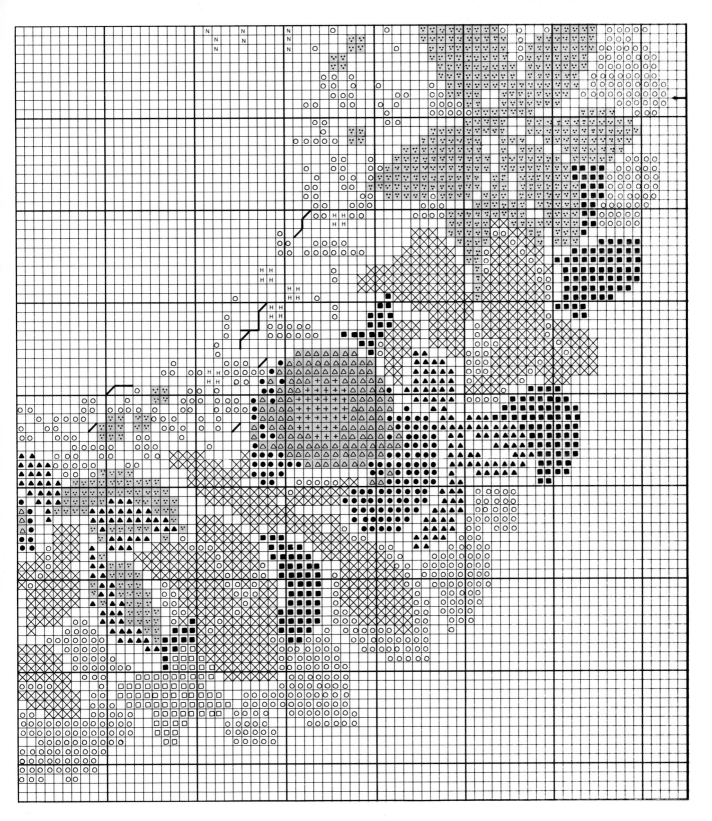

| 167 | $I$ | | | 598 | Turquoise-lt. |
| 168 | $\triangledown$ | | | 807 | Peacock Blue |
| 843 | ■ | | | 3364 | Pine Green |
| 875 | O | | | 503 | Blue Green-med. |
| 878 | X | | | 501 | Blue Green-dk. |
| 936 | E | $\mathcal{E}$ | | 632 | Pecan-dk. |

**Step 2:** Backstitch (1 strand)

| 922 | | | 930 | Antique Blue-dk. (in "M") |
| 936 | | | 632 | Pecan-dk. (stems) |

# Glorious Nativity

**SAMPLE**
Stitched on raw Belfast Linen 32 over 2 threads, the finished design size is 7⅝" x 15¾". The fabric was cut 14" x 22".

| FABRICS | DESIGN SIZES |
|---|---|
| Aida 11 | 11⅛" x 22⅞" |
| Aida 14 | 8¾" x 17⅞" |
| Aida 18 | 6¾" x 14" |
| Hardanger 22 | 5½" x 11⅜" |

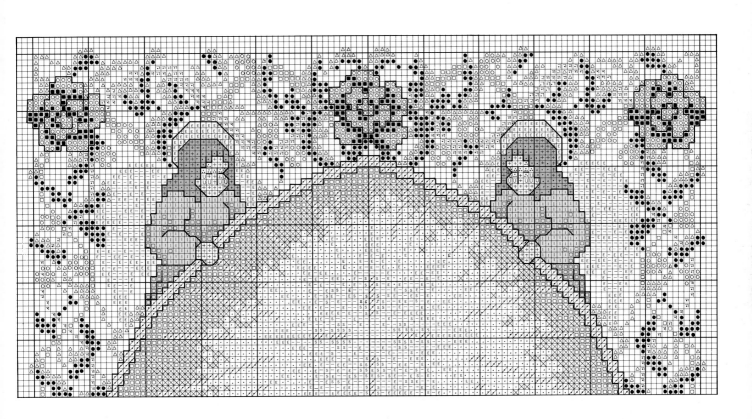

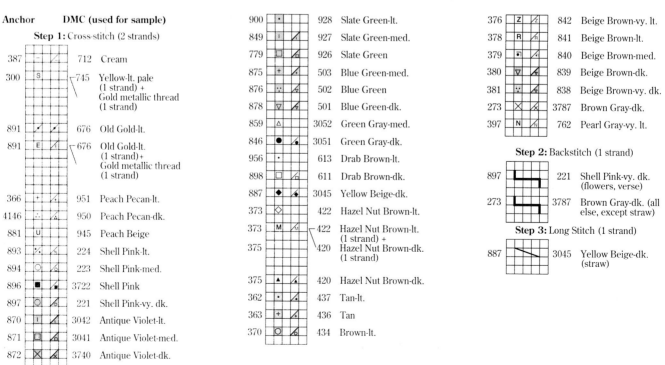

| Anchor | | DMC (used for sample) | |
|---|---|---|---|

**Step 1:** Cross-stitch (2 strands)

| 387 | | 712 | Cream |
|---|---|---|---|
| 300 | S | 745 | Yellow-lt. pale (1 strand) + Gold metallic thread (1 strand) |
| 891 | | 676 | Old Gold-lt. |
| 891 | E | 676 | Old Gold-lt. (1 strand) + Gold metallic thread (1 strand) |
| 366 | + | 951 | Peach Pecan-lt. |
| 4146 | | 950 | Peach Pecan-dk. |
| 881 | U | 945 | Peach Beige |
| 893 | | 224 | Shell Pink-lt. |
| 894 | O | 223 | Shell Pink-med. |
| 896 | ■ | 3722 | Shell Pink |
| 897 | O | 221 | Shell Pink-vy. dk. |
| 870 | I | 3042 | Antique Violet-lt. |
| 871 | □ | 3041 | Antique Violet-med. |
| 872 | X | 3740 | Antique Violet-dk. |
| 921 | X | 931 | Antique Blue-med. |

| 900 | • | 928 | Slate Green-lt. |
|---|---|---|---|
| 849 | I | 927 | Slate Green-med. |
| 779 | □ | 926 | Slate Green |
| 875 | + | 503 | Blue Green-med. |
| 876 | | 502 | Blue Green |
| 878 | ▽ | 501 | Blue Green-dk. |
| 859 | △ | 3052 | Green Gray-med. |
| 846 | ● | 3051 | Green Gray-dk. |
| 956 | • | 613 | Drab Brown-lt. |
| 898 | □ | 611 | Drab Brown-dk. |
| 887 | ◆ | 3045 | Yellow Beige-dk. |
| 373 | ◇ | 422 | Hazel Nut Brown-lt. |
| 373 | M | 422 | Hazel Nut Brown-lt. (1 strand) + |
| 375 | | 420 | Hazel Nut Brown-dk. (1 strand) |
| 375 | ▲ | 420 | Hazel Nut Brown-dk. |
| 362 | • | 437 | Tan-lt. |
| 363 | + | 436 | Tan |
| 370 | O | 434 | Brown-lt. |

| 376 | Z | 842 | Beige Brown-vy. lt. |
|---|---|---|---|
| 378 | R | 841 | Beige Brown-lt. |
| 379 | • | 840 | Beige Brown-med. |
| 380 | ▽ | 839 | Beige Brown-dk. |
| 381 | | 838 | Beige Brown-vy. dk. |
| 273 | X | 3787 | Brown Gray-dk. |
| 397 | N | 762 | Pearl Gray-vy. lt. |

**Step 2:** Backstitch (1 strand)

| 897 | | 221 | Shell Pink-vy. dk. (flowers, verse) |
|---|---|---|---|
| 273 | | 3787 | Brown Gray-dk. (all else, except straw) |

**Step 3:** Long Stitch (1 strand)

| 887 | | 3045 | Yellow Beige-dk. (straw) |
|---|---|---|---|

**Stitch Count: 122 x 251**

# Everyday Pleasures

*Everyday pleasures abound
in this diverse assortment of
designs. Decorate throughout
the year with botanical pillows
and framed pieces stitched in
rich spring and autumn colors.
Recapture special memories
with a family heirloom floral
mat, or add a whimsical touch
to a youngster's room with
Lewis Carroll's perennially
late rabbit.*

# Family Heirloom

## SAMPLE

Stitched on cream Aida 14 over 1 thread, the finished design size is 11¼" x 13¼". The fabric was cut 18" x 20".

| FABRICS | DESIGN SIZES |
|---------|--------------|
| Aida 11 | 14¼" x 17" |
| Aida 18 | 8¾" x 10¼" |
| Hardanger 22 | 7¼" x 8½" |

## MATERIALS

Completed cross-stitch on cream Aida 14
Professionally cut mat (see Step 1)
Dressmaker's pen
Double-sided tape
Masking tape

## DIRECTIONS

**1.** Have a professional framer cut mat board. Outside dimensions are 14½" x 16¾". Window dimensions are 7¼" x 9¼".

**2.** With design centered, trim Aida to measure 16½" x 18¼".

**3.** Place Aida wrong side up on flat surface. Center mat over fabric and, using dressmaker's pen, trace edge of window onto fabric. Then draw a smaller window 2" inside first window. Cut along inside traced line. Clip corners between 2 traced lines at a 45° angle.

**4.** On wrong side of mat, run a strip of double-sided tape along top edge of window. Fold fabric over mat, making sure that violet cross-stitched border is parallel to inside edge of mat.

**5.** Repeat Step 4 for bottom edge of window and then sides.

**6.** Still on wrong side of mat, run a strip of double-sided tape along top outside edge to within 2" of corners. Fold fabric over edge, pulling it taut. Repeat along bottom edge and then sides. Trim excess fabric from corners on back and secure with masking tape. Place mat in a ready-made frame or have a professional framer complete framing.

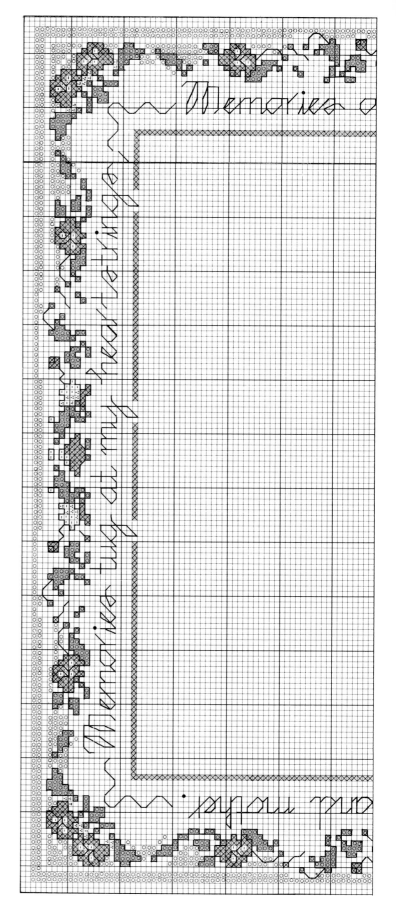

| Anchor | | DMC (used for sample) | |
|--------|--|------|--|
| **Step 1:** Cross-stitch (2 strands) | | | |
| 293 | O | 727 | Topaz-vy. lt. |
| 297 | - | 743 | Yellow-med. |
| 303 | ∴ | 742 | Tangerine-lt. |
| 95 | X ╱ | 554 | Violet-lt. |
| 213 | ◎ | 369 | Pistachio Green-vy. lt. |
| 214 | X | 368 | Pistachio Green-lt. |
| **Step 2:** Backstitch (1 strand) | | | |
| 871 | | 3041 | Antique Violet-med. (flowers) |
| 862 | | 935 | Avocado Green-dk. (letters) |
| **Step 3:** French Knot (1 strand) | | | |
| 862 | ● | 935 | Avocado Green-dk. |

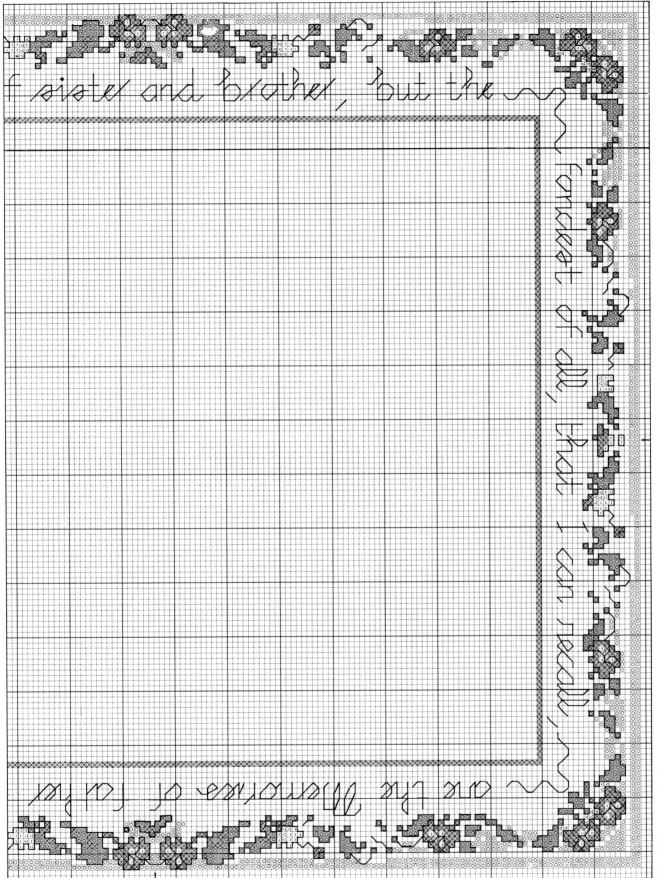

sister and brother, but the

fondest of all that I can recall

are the memories of Father

Stitch Count: 158 x 186

# No Time to Spare

**SAMPLE**
Stitched on white Belfast Linen 32 over 2 threads, the finished
design size is 9½" x 4½". The fabric was cut 16" x 11".

| FABRICS | DESIGN SIZES |
|---|---|
| Aida 11 | 13⅞" x 6⅝" |
| Aida 14 | 10⅞" x 5¼" |
| Aida 18 | 8½" x 4" |
| Hardanger 22 | 6⅞" x 3⅜" |

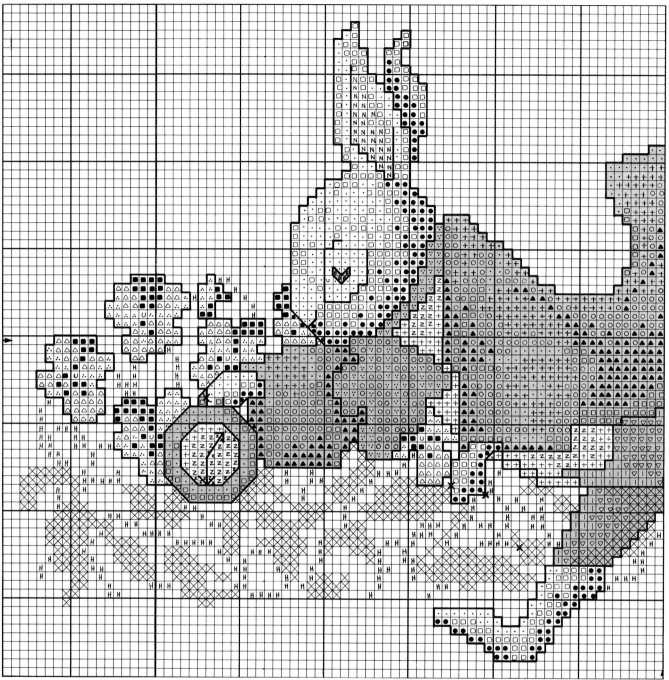

**Stitch Count: 152 x 73**

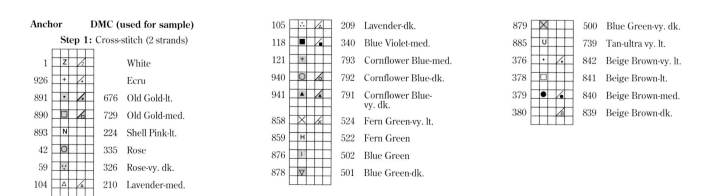

| Anchor | | DMC (used for sample) |
|---|---|---|
| | | **Step 1:** Cross-stitch (2 strands) |

| Anchor | | | DMC | |
|---|---|---|---|---|
| 1 | Z / | | | White |
| 926 | + / | | | Ecru |
| 891 | · / | | 676 | Old Gold-lt. |
| 890 | □ / | | 729 | Old Gold-med. |
| 893 | N | | 224 | Shell Pink-lt. |
| 42 | O | | 335 | Rose |
| 59 | ·: | | 326 | Rose-vy. dk. |
| 104 | △ / | | 210 | Lavender-med. |

| Anchor | | | DMC | |
|---|---|---|---|---|
| 105 | ·: / | | 209 | Lavender-dk. |
| 118 | ■ / | | 340 | Blue Violet-med. |
| 121 | + | | 793 | Cornflower Blue-med. |
| 940 | O / | | 792 | Cornflower Blue-dk. |
| 941 | ▲ / | | 791 | Cornflower Blue-vy. dk. |
| 858 | X / | | 524 | Fern Green-vy. lt. |
| 859 | H | | 522 | Fern Green |
| 876 | I | | 502 | Blue Green |
| 878 | ▽ | | 501 | Blue Green-dk. |

| Anchor | | | DMC | |
|---|---|---|---|---|
| 879 | X / | | 500 | Blue Green-vy. dk. |
| 885 | U | | 739 | Tan-ultra vy. lt. |
| 376 | · / | | 842 | Beige Brown-vy. lt. |
| 378 | □ | | 841 | Beige Brown-lt. |
| 379 | ● / | | 840 | Beige Brown-med. |
| 380 | B | | 839 | Beige Brown-dk. |

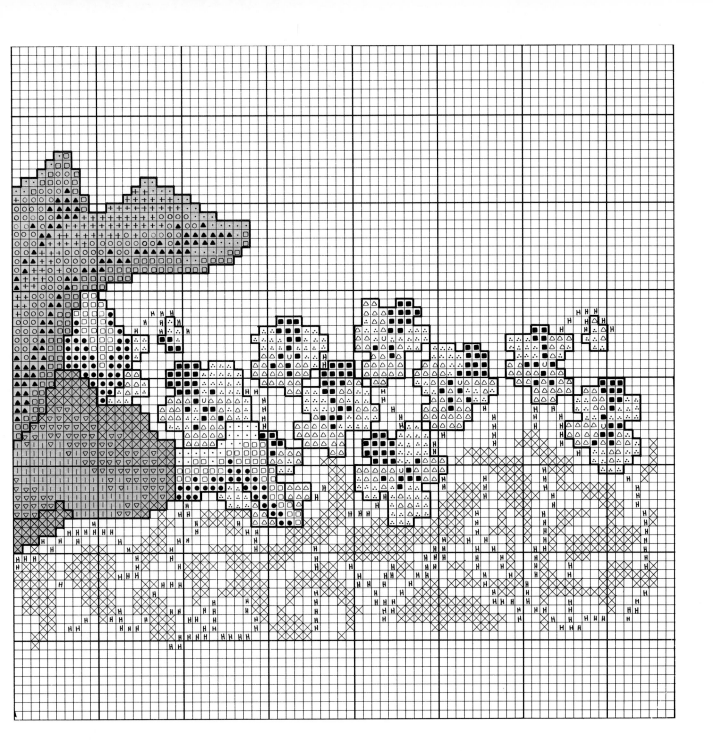

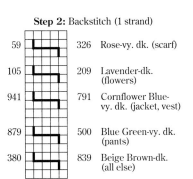

**Step 2:** Backstitch (1 strand)

| | | |
|---|---|---|
| 59 | 326 | Rose-vy. dk. (scarf) |
| 105 | 209 | Lavender-dk. (flowers) |
| 941 | 791 | Cornflower Blue-vy. dk. (jacket, vest) |
| 879 | 500 | Blue Green-vy. dk. (pants) |
| 380 | 839 | Beige Brown-dk. (all else) |

**Step 3:** Long Stitch (1 strand)

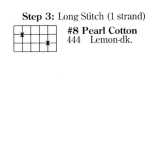

**#8 Pearl Cotton**
444   Lemon-dk.

# Floral Tapestry Trio

**Stitch Count: 92 x 92  (Design 1)**

**Stitch Count: 93 x 93 (Design 2)**

**Stitch Count: 92 x 92  (Design 3)**

## SAMPLE for Design 1

Stitched on cream Aida 11 over 1 thread, the finished design size is 8⅜" x 8⅜".
The fabric was cut 12" x 12". *Note:* Four strands of DMC floss equal 2 strands
of Medicis wool.

| FABRICS | DESIGN SIZES |
|---------|--------------|
| Aida 14 | 6⅝" x 6⅝" |
| Aida 18 | 5⅛" x 5⅛" |
| Hardanger 22 | 4⅛" x 4⅛" |

## SAMPLE for Design 2

Stitched on cream Aida 11 over 1 thread, the finished design size 8½" x 8½".
The fabric was cut 12" x 12". *Note:* Four strands of DMC floss equal 2 strands
of Medicis wool.

| FABRICS | DESIGN SIZES |
|---------|--------------|
| Aida 14 | 6⅝" x 6⅝" |
| Aida 18 | 5⅛" x 5⅛" |
| Hardanger 22 | 4¼" x 4¼" |

## SAMPLE for Design 3

Stitched on cream Aida 11 over 1 thread, the finished design size is 8⅜" x 8⅜".
The fabric was cut 12" x 12". *Note*: Four strands of DMC floss equal 2 strands
of Medicis wool.

| FABRICS | DESIGN SIZES |
|---------|--------------|
| Aida 14 | 6⅝" x 6⅝" |
| Aida 18 | 5⅛" x 5⅛" |
| Hardanger 22 | 4⅛" x 4⅛" |

## Design 1

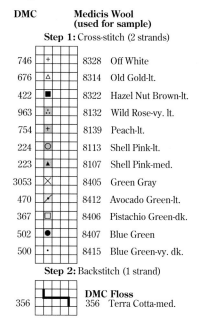

**DMC** — **Medicis Wool** (used for sample)

**Step 1:** Cross-stitch (2 strands)

| DMC | | Medicis Wool | |
|-----|---|------|---|
| 746 | + | 8328 | Off White |
| 676 | △ | 8314 | Old Gold-lt. |
| 422 | ■ | 8322 | Hazel Nut Brown-lt. |
| 963 | ∴ | 8132 | Wild Rose-vy. lt. |
| 754 | + | 8139 | Peach-lt. |
| 224 | ○ | 8113 | Shell Pink-lt. |
| 223 | ▲ | 8107 | Shell Pink-med. |
| 3053 | ✕ | 8405 | Green Gray |
| 470 | ╱ | 8412 | Avocado Green-lt. |
| 367 | □ | 8406 | Pistachio Green-dk. |
| 502 | ● | 8407 | Blue Green |
| 500 | · | 8415 | Blue Green-vy. dk. |

**Step 2:** Backstitch (1 strand)

| 356 | | **DMC Floss** 356 Terra Cotta-med. |

## Design 2

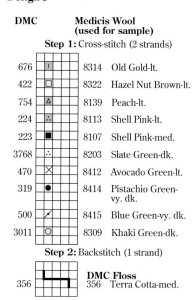

**DMC** — **Medicis Wool** (used for sample)

**Step 1:** Cross-stitch (2 strands)

| DMC | | Medicis Wool | |
|-----|---|------|---|
| 676 | I | 8314 | Old Gold-lt. |
| 422 | ∴ | 8322 | Hazel Nut Brown-lt. |
| 963 | B | 8132 | Wild Rose-vy. lt. |
| 754 | ◩ | 8139 | Peach-lt. |
| 224 | + | 8113 | Shell Pink-lt. |
| 223 | ● | 8107 | Shell Pink-med. |
| 315 | U | 8122 | Antique Mauve-vy. dk. |
| 800 | ∴ | 8800 | Delft-pale |
| 3348 | △ | 8420 | Yellow Green-lt. |
| 3053 | E | 8405 | Green Gray |
| 470 | ▲ | 8412 | Avocado Green-lt. |
| 367 | ○ | 8406 | Pistachio Green-dk. |
| 319 | □ | 8414 | Pistachio Green-vy. dk. |
| 502 | ■ | 8407 | Blue Green |
| 500 | ✕ | 8415 | Blue Green-vy. dk. |
| 3032 | ╱ | 8307 | Mocha Brown-med. |

**Step 2:** Backstitch (1 strand)

| 356 | | **DMC Floss** 356 Terra Cotta-med. |

## Design 3

**DMC** — **Medicis Wool** (used for sample)

**Step 1:** Cross-stitch (2 strands)

| DMC | | Medicis Wool | |
|-----|---|------|---|
| 676 | I | 8314 | Old Gold-lt. |
| 422 | □ | 8322 | Hazel Nut Brown-lt. |
| 754 | △ | 8139 | Peach-lt. |
| 224 | ∴ | 8113 | Shell Pink-lt. |
| 223 | ■ | 8107 | Shell Pink-med. |
| 3768 | ∴ | 8203 | Slate Green-dk. |
| 470 | ✕ | 8412 | Avocado Green-lt. |
| 319 | ● | 8414 | Pistachio Green-vy. dk. |
| 500 | ╱ | 8415 | Blue Green-vy. dk. |
| 3011 | ○ | 8309 | Khaki Green-dk. |

**Step 2:** Backstitch (1 strand)

| 356 | | **DMC Floss** 356 Terra Cotta-med. |

**MATERIALS** (for 1 pillow)
Completed cross-stitch on cream Aida 11
¼ yard of coordinating fabric for back; matching thread
⅜ yard of contrasting fabric for corded piping; matching thread
1 yard of medium cording
Stuffing

**DIRECTIONS**
All seam allowances are ¼".

1. Trim design piece (pillow front) to ¼" outside all edges of design. Using pillow front as a pattern, cut pillow back from coordinating fabric. From contrasting fabric, cut 1½"-wide bias strips, piecing as needed to equal 36". With bias strip and cording, make 36" of corded piping.

2. With right sides facing and raw edges aligned, stitch piping around pillow front, stitching close to edges of stitched design. With right sides facing and raw edges aligned, stitch pillow front to pillow back, sewing along stitching line of piping and leaving an opening for turning. Trim corners and turn. Stuff firmly. Slipstitch opening closed.

# Birds and Flowers

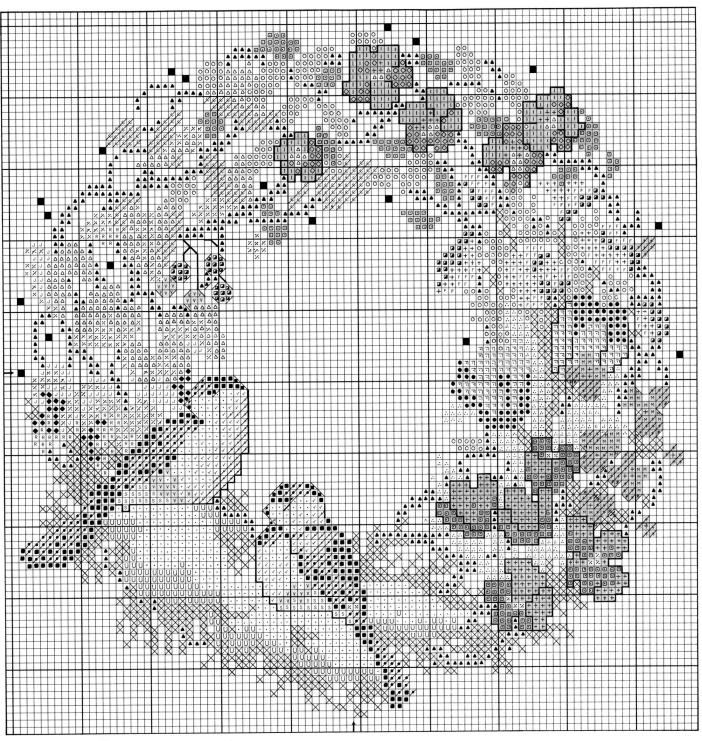

**Stitch Count: 96 x 97**

## SAMPLE

Stitched on cream Belfast Linen 32 over 2 threads, the finished design size is 6" x 6". The fabric was cut 12" x 12". See Suppliers for Mill Hill Beads.

| FABRICS | DESIGN SIZES |
|---|---|
| Aida 11 | 8¾" x 8⅞" |
| Aida 14 | 6⅞" x 6⅞" |
| Aida 18 | 5⅜" x 5⅜" |
| Hardanger 22 | 4⅜" x 4⅜" |

**Anchor**  **DMC (used for sample)**

**Step 1:** Cross-stitch (2 strands)

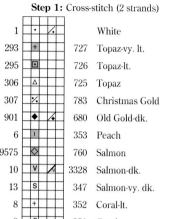

| Anchor | | DMC | |
|---|---|---|---|
| 1 | | | White |
| 293 | | 727 | Topaz-vy. lt. |
| 295 | | 726 | Topaz-lt. |
| 306 | | 725 | Topaz |
| 307 | | 783 | Christmas Gold |
| 901 | | 680 | Old Gold-dk. |
| 6 | | 353 | Peach |
| 9575 | | 760 | Salmon |
| 10 | | 3328 | Salmon-dk. |
| 13 | | 347 | Salmon-vy. dk. |
| 8 | | 352 | Coral-lt. |
| 9 | | 351 | Coral |
| 11 | | 350 | Coral-med. |
| 76 | | 961 | Wild Rose-dk. |
| 42 | | 309 | Rose-deep |
| 98 | | 553 | Violet-med. |
| 101 | | 327 | Antique Violet-vy. dk. |
| 128 | | 800 | Delft-pale |
| 874 | | 833 | Olive Green-lt. |
| 266 | | 3347 | Yellow Green-med. |
| 244 | | 987 | Forest Green-dk. |
| 215 | | 320 | Pistachio Green-med. |
| 246 | | 319 | Pistachio Green-vy. dk. |
| 307 | | 977 | Golden Brown-lt. |
| 308 | | 976 | Golden Brown-med. |
| 387 | | 822 | Beige Gray-lt. |
| 830 | | 644 | Beige Gray-med. |
| 379 | | 840 | Beige Brown-med. |
| 381 | | 838 | Beige Brown-vy. dk. |
| 382 | | 3371 | Black Brown |

**Step 2:** Backstitch (1 strand)

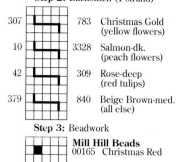

| | | | |
|---|---|---|---|
| 307 | | 783 | Christmas Gold (yellow flowers) |
| 10 | | 3328 | Salmon-dk. (peach flowers) |
| 42 | | 309 | Rose-deep (red tulips) |
| 379 | | 840 | Beige Brown-med. (all else) |

**Step 3:** Beadwork

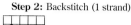

**Mill Hill Beads**
00165   Christmas Red

# Autumn Beauty

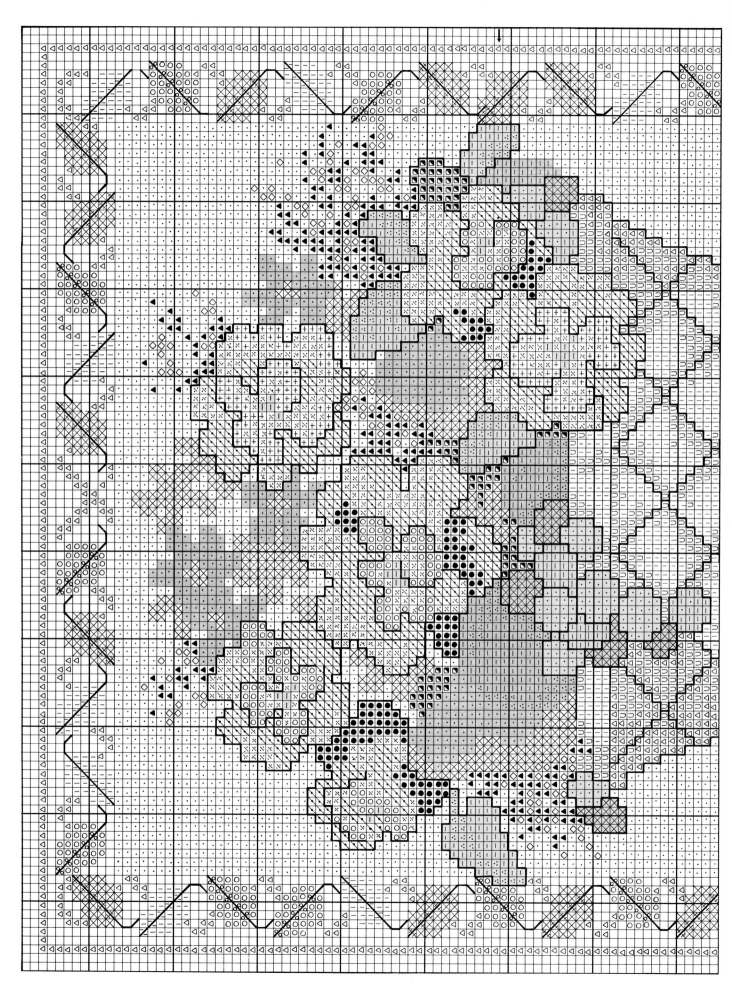

90

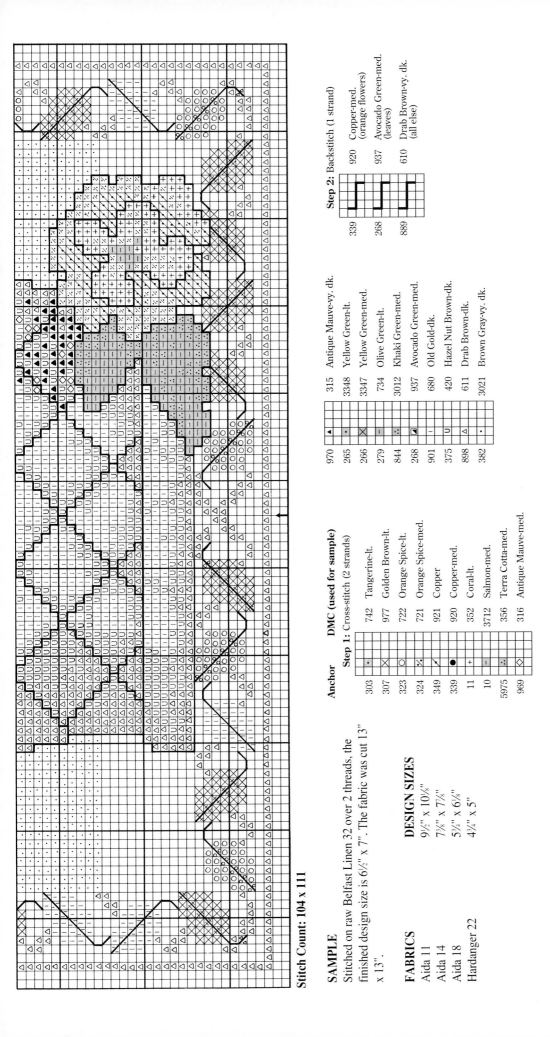

**Stitch Count: 104 x 111**

**Step 2:** Backstitch (1 strand)

| | | |
|---|---|---|
| 339 | 920 | Copper-med. (orange flowers) |
| 268 | 937 | Avocado Green-med. (leaves) |
| 889 | 610 | Drab Brown-vy. dk. (all else) |

| Anchor | | DMC | |
|---|---|---|---|
| 970 | ▲ | 315 | Antique Mauve-vy. dk. |
| 265 | · | 3348 | Yellow Green-lt. |
| 266 | X | 3347 | Yellow Green-med. |
| 279 | − | 734 | Olive Green-lt. |
| 844 | ∴ | 3012 | Khaki Green-med. |
| 268 | ◪ | 937 | Avocado Green-med. |
| 901 | – | 680 | Old Gold-dk. |
| 375 | U | 420 | Hazel Nut Brown-dk. |
| 898 | △ | 611 | Drab Brown-dk. |
| 382 | · | 3021 | Brown Gray-vy. dk. |

**Anchor**  **DMC (used for sample)**

**Step 1:** Cross-stitch (2 strands)

| | | | |
|---|---|---|---|
| 303 | · | 742 | Tangerine-lt. |
| 307 | X | 977 | Golden Brown-lt. |
| 323 | O | 722 | Orange Spice-lt. |
| 324 | ⊠ | 721 | Orange Spice-med. |
| 349 | ↗ | 921 | Copper |
| 339 | ● | 920 | Copper-med. |
| 11 | + | 352 | Coral-lt. |
| 10 | I | 3712 | Salmon-med. |
| 5975 | ∴ | 356 | Terra Cotta-med. |
| 969 | ◇ | 316 | Antique Mauve-med. |

**SAMPLE**

Stitched on raw Belfast Linen 32 over 2 threads, the finished design size is 6½" x 7". The fabric was cut 13" x 13".

| FABRICS | DESIGN SIZES |
|---|---|
| Aida 11 | 9½" x 10⅛" |
| Aida 14 | 7⅞" x 7⅞" |
| Aida 18 | 5¾" x 6⅛" |
| Hardanger 22 | 4¾" x 5" |

# Christmas Towels

**SAMPLE for Towels**
Stitched on deep teal or rich cranberry Christmas Fingertip Towel 14 over 1 thread. For each towel, stitch 2 side sections and 1 center section. See Suppliers for towels.

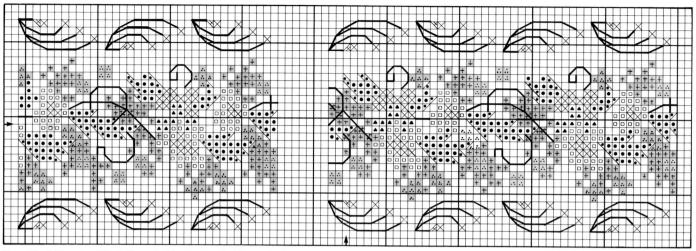

**Deep Teal Floral**    Stitch Count: 36 x 28 (for 1 side section)

Stitch Count: 48 x 28 (for center section)

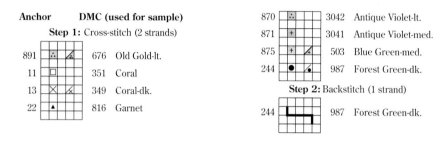

| Anchor | | DMC (used for sample) | |
|--------|--|------|--|
| | **Step 1:** Cross-stitch (2 strands) | | |
| 891 | | 676 | Old Gold-lt. |
| 11 | | 351 | Coral |
| 13 | | 349 | Coral-dk. |
| 22 | | 816 | Garnet |

| | | | |
|---|---|---|---|
| 870 | | 3042 | Antique Violet-lt. |
| 871 | | 3041 | Antique Violet-med. |
| 875 | | 503 | Blue Green-med. |
| 244 | | 987 | Forest Green-dk. |
| | **Step 2:** Backstitch (1 strand) | | |
| 244 | | 987 | Forest Green-dk. |

**Deep Teal with Hearts**    Stitch Count: 36 x 28 (for 1 side section)

Stitch Count: 48 x 28 (for center section)

| Anchor | | DMC (used for sample) | |
|--------|--|------|--|
| | **Step 1:** Cross-stitch (2 strands) | | |
| 890 | | 729 | Old Gold-med. |
| 901 | | 680 | Old Gold-dk. |
| 47 | | 321 | Christmas Red |
| 20 | | 498 | Christmas Red-dk. |
| 43 | | 815 | Garnet-med. |
| 216 | | 367 | Pistachio Green-dk. |

**Step 2:** Backstitch (1 strand)

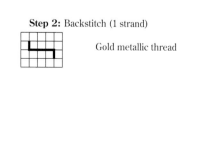

Gold metallic thread

**Deep Teal Fleur-de-lis**   Stitch Count: 36 x 28 (for 1 side section)   Stitch Count: 48 x 28 (for center section)

| Anchor | | DMC (used for sample) |
|---|---|---|

**Step 1:** Cross-stitch (2 strands)

| 891 | Old Gold-lt. | 676 |
|---|---|---|
| 890 | Old Gold-med. | 729 |
| 47 | Christmas Red-med. | 304 |
| 22 | Garnet | 816 |

**Step 2:** Backstitch (1 strand)

Gold metallic thread

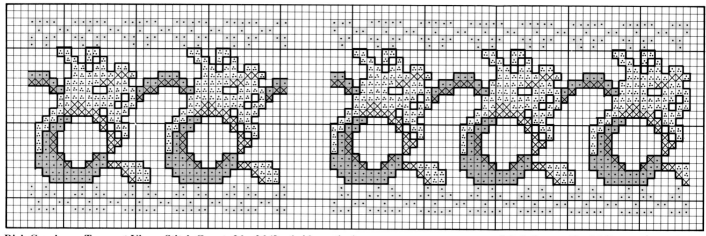

**Rich Cranberry Trumpet Vine**   Stitch Count: 36 x 26 (for 1 side section)

Stitch Count: 50 x 26 (for center section)

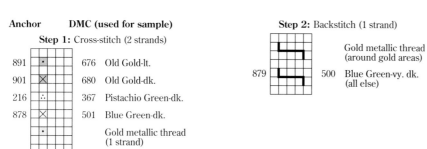

| Anchor | | DMC (used for sample) | |
|---|---|---|---|
| | **Step 1:** Cross-stitch (2 strands) | | |
| 891 | | 676 | Old Gold-lt. |
| 901 | | 680 | Old Gold-dk. |
| 216 | | 367 | Pistachio Green-dk. |
| 878 | | 501 | Blue Green-dk. |
| | | | Gold metallic thread (1 strand) |

**Step 2:** Backstitch (1 strand)

Gold metallic thread (around gold areas)

| 879 | | 500 | Blue Green-vy. dk. (all else) |
|---|---|---|---|

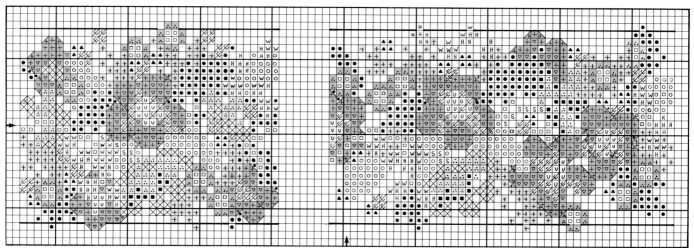

**Rich Cranberry Floral**   Stitch Count: 36 x 28 (for 1 side section)

Stitch Count: 48 x 28 (for center section)

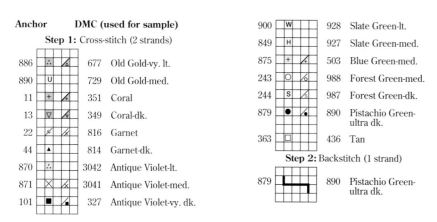

| Anchor | | DMC (used for sample) | |
|---|---|---|---|
| | **Step 1:** Cross-stitch (2 strands) | | |
| 886 | | 677 | Old Gold-vy. lt. |
| 890 | U | 729 | Old Gold-med. |
| 11 | + | 351 | Coral |
| 13 | ▽ | 349 | Coral-dk. |
| 22 | | 816 | Garnet |
| 44 | ▲ | 814 | Garnet-dk. |
| 870 | | 3042 | Antique Violet-lt. |
| 871 | ✕ | 3041 | Antique Violet-med. |
| 101 | ■ | 327 | Antique Violet-vy. dk. |

| 900 | W | 928 | Slate Green-lt. |
|---|---|---|---|
| 849 | H | 927 | Slate Green-med. |
| 875 | + | 503 | Blue Green-med. |
| 243 | ○ | 988 | Forest Green-med. |
| 244 | S | 987 | Forest Green-dk. |
| 879 | ● | 890 | Pistachio Green-ultra dk. |
| 363 | □ | 436 | Tan |

**Step 2:** Backstitch (1 strand)

| 879 | | 890 | Pistachio Green-ultra dk. |
|---|---|---|---|

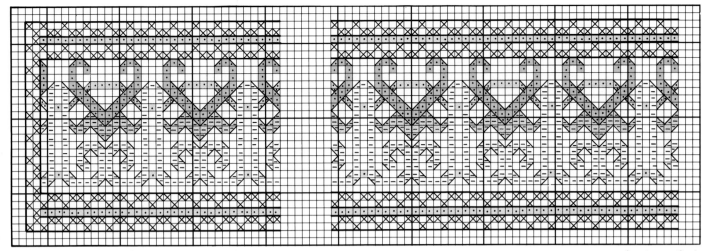

**Rich Cranberry with Gold Geometric (left section)**                                              **(center section)**

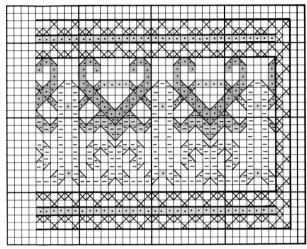

**(right section) Stitch Count: 132 x 28 (for complete design)**

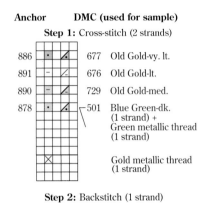

| Anchor | | DMC (used for sample) | |
|---|---|---|---|
| **Step 1:** Cross-stitch (2 strands) | | | |
| 886 | · / | 677 | Old Gold-vy. lt. |
| 891 | − / | 676 | Old Gold-lt. |
| 890 | − / | 729 | Old Gold-med. |
| 878 | · / | 501 | Blue Green-dk. (1 strand) + Green metallic thread (1 strand) |
| | ✕ | | Gold metallic thread (1 strand) |

**Step 2:** Backstitch (1 strand)

Gold metallic thread

97

# Capture The Holiday Spirit

The holiday spirit is yours to keep — and to share — when you focus on these four popular holidays. First, dress up your home with pillows: Bright spring flowers spell out "Happy Easter," and flags from the early years of our nation mark Independence Day. A Halloween windsock will add a bewitching chill to the air. And together for the first time are all seven of our beloved Father Christmases.

# Happy Easter

**Stitch Count: 155 x 95**

| Anchor | | DMC (used for sample) | |
|---|---|---|---|
| | | **Step 1: Cross-stitch (2 strands)** | |
| 1 | | | White |
| 386 | + | 746 | Off White |
| 301 | U | 744 | Yellow-pale |
| 303 | · | 742 | Tangerine-lt. |
| 891 | M | 676 | Old Gold-lt. |
| 329 | | 3340 | Apricot-med. |
| 25 | I | 3708 | Melon-lt. |
| 26 | □ | 894 | Carnation-vy. lt. |
| 35 | H | 891 | Carnation-dk. |
| 35 | J | 891 | Carnation-dk. (1strand) + |
| 329 | | 3340 | Apricot-med. (1 strand) |
| 59 | ▲ | 326 | Rose-vy. dk. |
| 76 | ⊠ | 603 | Cranberry |
| 85 | G | 3609 | Plum-ultra lt. |
| 88 | + | 718 | Plum |
| 69 | ○ | 3687 | Mauve |
| 70 | | 3685 | Mauve-dk. |
| 95 | N | 554 | Violet-lt. |
| 98 | △ | 553 | Violet-med. |
| 117 | R | 341 | Blue Violet-lt. |
| 119 | ■ | 333 | Blue Violet-dk. |
| 900 | – | 928 | Slate Green-lt. |
| 849 | B | 927 | Slate Green-med. |
| 265 | S | 3348 | Yellow Green-lt. |
| 266 | □ | 3347 | Yellow Green-med. |
| 216 | ⨯ | 367 | Pistachio Green-dk. |
| 209 | ○ | 913 | Nile Green-med. |
| 228 | | 910 | Emerald Green-dk. |
| 187 | ▽ | 992 | Aquamarine |
| 189 | ● | 991 | Aquamarine-dk. |

**Step 2: Backstitch (1 strand)**

| 901 | | 680 | Old Gold-dk. (daffodils) |
|---|---|---|---|
| 69 | | 3687 | Mauve (tulips) |
| 921 | | 931 | Antique Blue-med. (lilies, sweet peas) |
| 216 | | 367 | Pistachio Green-dk. (all else) |

**Step 3: Smyrna Cross-stitch (1 strand)**

| 921 | ✳ | 931 | Antique Blue-med. |
|---|---|---|---|

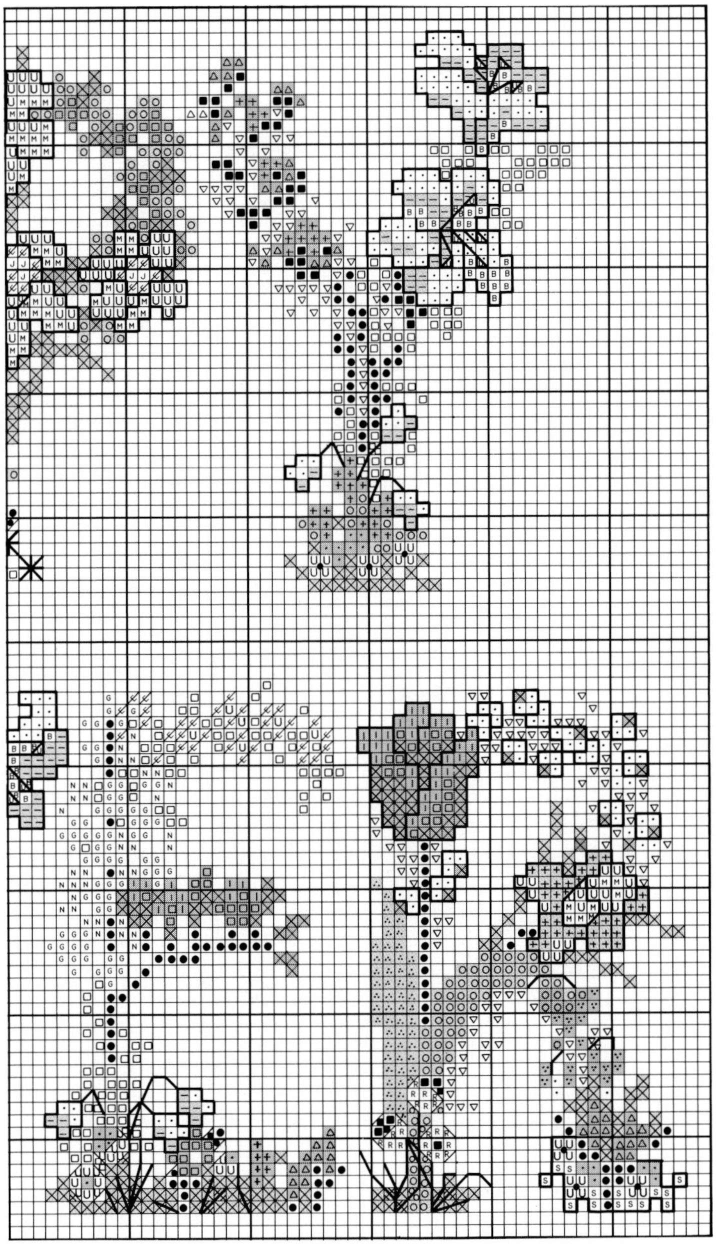

**Step 4:** French Knot (1 strand)

216 ● 367 Pistachio Green-dk.

## SAMPLE

Stitched on moss green Lugana 25 over 2 threads, the finished design size is 12⅜" x 7⅝". The fabric was cut 20" x 14".

| FABRICS | DESIGN SIZES |
|---|---|
| Aida 11 | 14⅛" x 8⅝" |
| Aida 14 | 11⅛" x 6¾" |
| Aida 18 | 8⅝" x 5¼" |
| Hardanger 22 | 7" x 4⅜" |

## MATERIALS

Completed cross-stitch on moss green Lugana 25; matching thread
½ yard of unstitched moss green Lugana 25 for pillow back
1¼ yards of print fabric
4 yards (¼"-diameter) cording
½ yard of fleece
Stuffing

## DIRECTIONS

All seam allowances are ¼".

**1.** With design centered, trim Lugana to 17" x 13". From remaining Lugana, cut a 17" x 13" piece for pillow back. From fleece, cut 2 (17" x 13") pieces. Pin fleece to wrong side of front and back pieces. Zigzag edges together. Press as needed to keep smooth.

**2.** To make corded piping and tubing, cut 1"-wide bias strips from printed fabric, piecing as needed to equal 4 yards. Make 60" of corded piping and 83" of corded tubing. Cut tubing into 1 (35") piece and 4 (12") pieces.

**3.** With right sides facing and raw edges aligned, stitch piping to right side of design piece. With right sides facing, stitch design piece to pillow back on stitching line of piping, leaving an opening for turning. Clip corners. Turn.

**4.** To make loops on top edge of pillow, mark center of 35" piece of corded tubing. Make a 2½" loop. Slipstitch loop to center top of pillow. Working to the right, make 3 more loops, decreasing in size and ending 5½" from corner. Slipstitch in place. Repeat for 3 loops on left side.

**5.** Stuff pillow firmly. Slipstitch opening closed.

**6.** For corner bow, use 1 (12") piece of corded tubing. Make 1½" loops (see Diagram). Tack loops securely. Repeat to make 3 more bows. Slipstitch a bow to each corner.

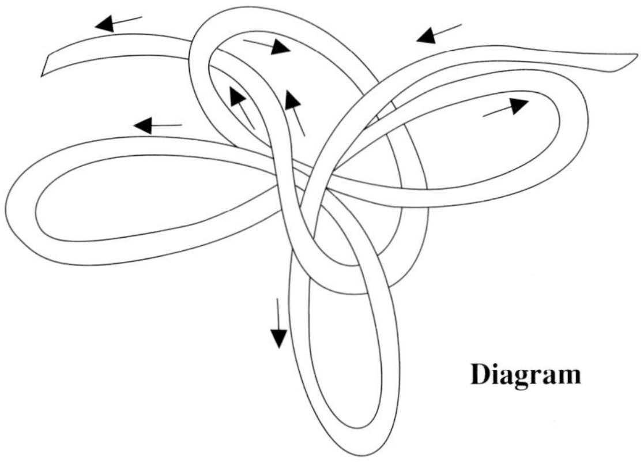

**Diagram**

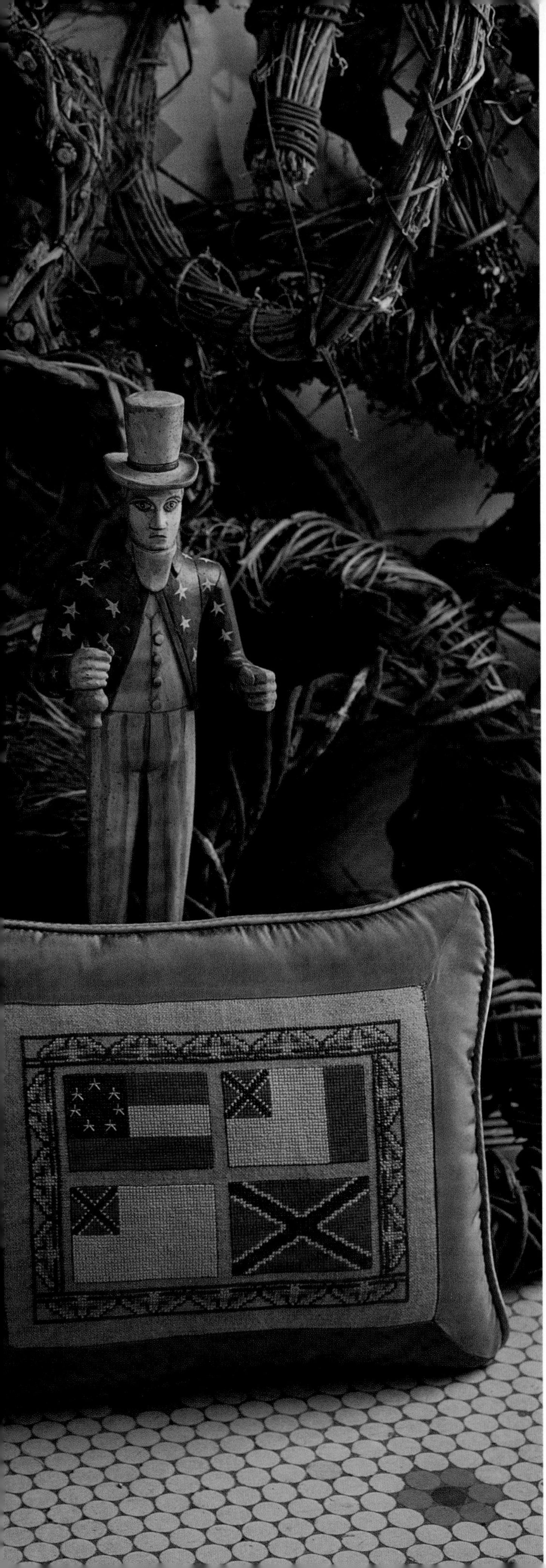

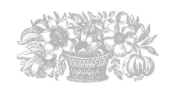

# *Patriotic Pillows*

**SAMPLE for Liberty Flag Pillow**
Stitched on natural Dirty Linen 26 over 2 threads, the finished design size is 9¼" x 6⅞". The fabric was cut 16" x 13".

| **FABRICS** | **DESIGN SIZES** |
|---|---|
| Aida 11 | 11" x 8⅛" |
| Aida 14 | 8⅝" x 6⅜" |
| Aida 18 | 6¾" x 5" |
| Hardanger 22 | 5½" x 4" |

**SAMPLE for Stars and Stripes Pillow**
Stitched on natural Dirty Linen 26 over 2 threads, the finished design size is 9½" x 7". The fabric was cut 16" x 13".

| **FABRICS** | **DESIGN SIZES** |
|---|---|
| Aida 11 | 11⅛" x 8¼" |
| Aida 14 | 8¾" x 6½" |
| Aida 18 | 6⅞" x 5" |
| Hardanger 22 | 5⅝" x 4⅛" |

**SAMPLE for Confederate Pillow**
Stitched on natural Dirty Linen 26 over 2 threads, the finished design size is 9½" x 7". The fabric was cut 16" x 13".

| **FABRICS** | **DESIGN SIZES** |
|---|---|
| Aida 11 | 11⅛" x 8¼" |
| Aida 14 | 8¾" x 6½" |
| Aida 18 | 6⅞" x 5" |
| Hardanger 22 | 5⅝" x 4⅛" |

## MATERIALS (for 1 pillow)

Completed cross-stitch on natural Dirty Linen 26
1 yard (45"-wide) bronze satin fabric; matching thread
1½ yards (¼"-diameter) cording
½ yard of fleece
Stuffing

## DIRECTIONS

All seam allowances are ¼".

**1.** With design centered, trim linen to 11" x 8½". From fleece, cut 2 (15½" x 12½") pieces. From satin fabric, cut 1 (15½" x 12½") piece for pillow back, 2 (16" x 3") pieces for top and bottom borders, and 2 (13" x 3") pieces for side borders. Also, from satin fabric, cut 1¼"-wide bias strips, piecing as needed to equal 1½ yards. With bias strips and cording, make corded piping.

**2.** Mark center of each edge of design piece and 1 long edge of each border strip. With right sides facing, center marks matching, and raw edges aligned, stitch 1 border strip to design piece. Stitch to within ¼" of each corner; backstitch. Repeat to join remaining border strips. Press seams toward borders.

**3.** To miter corners, fold right sides of 2 adjacent border strips together and stitch at a 45° angle (see Diagram). Trim seam allowance to ¼". Repeat for remaining corners.

**4.** Pin fleece to wrong side of front and back pieces. Zigzag edges together. Press as needed to keep smooth.

**5.** With right sides facing and raw edges aligned, stitch piping to pillow front. With right sides facing, stitch pillow front to back, sewing on stitching line of piping and leaving an opening for turning. Clip corners and turn. Stuff pillow firmly. Slipstitch opening closed.

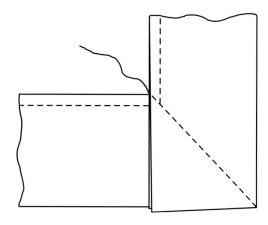

**Diagram**

### Liberty Flag Pillow

| Anchor | | DMC (used for sample) | |
|---|---|---|---|
| **Step 1:** Cross-stitch (2 strands) | | | |
| 885 | · ◢ | 739 | Tan-ultra vy. lt. |
| 887 | ·· | 3046 | Yellow Beige-med. |
| 373 | △ | 3045 | Yellow Beige-dk. |
| 13 | ● | 347 | Salmon-vy. dk. |
| 922 | · ◢ | 930 | Antique Blue-dk. |
| 861 | ■ ◣ | 3363 | Pine Green-med. |
| **Step 2:** Backstitch (1 strand) | | | |
| 885 | | 739 | Tan-ultra vy. lt. (stars) |
| 149 | | 311 | Navy Blue-med. (lettering, flag outlines) |
| 861 | | 3363 | Pine Green-med. (tree trunk) |

### Stars and Stripes Pillow

| Anchor | | DMC (used for sample) | |
|---|---|---|---|
| **Step 1:** Cross-stitch (2 strands) | | | |
| 885 | · | 739 | Tan-ultra vy. lt. |
| 887 | ·· | 3046 | Yellow Beige-med. |
| 373 | △ | 3045 | Yellow Beige-dk. |
| 13 | · | 347 | Salmon-vy. dk. |
| 920 | ○ | 932 | Antique Blue-lt. |
| 922 | ✕ | 930 | Antique Blue-dk. |
| **Step 2:** Backstitch (1 strand) | | | |
| 885 | | 739 | Tan-ultra vy. lt. (star circle, tan lettering) |
| 149 | | 311 | Navy Blue-med. (all else) |

### Confederate Pillow

| Anchor | | DMC (used for sample) | |
|---|---|---|---|
| **Step 1:** Cross-stitch (2 strands) | | | |
| 885 | · | 739 | Tan-ultra vy. lt. |
| 887 | ·· | 3046 | Yellow Beige-med. |
| 373 | △ | 3045 | Yellow Beige-dk. |
| 13 | · | 347 | Salmon-vy. dk. |
| 922 | ✕ | 930 | Antique Blue-dk. |
| 889 | □ | 610 | Drab Brown-vy. dk. |
| **Step 2:** Backstitch (1 strand) | | | |
| 885 | | 739 | Tan-ultra vy. lt. (2 strands) (stars) |
| 149 | | 311 | Navy Blue-med. (all else) |

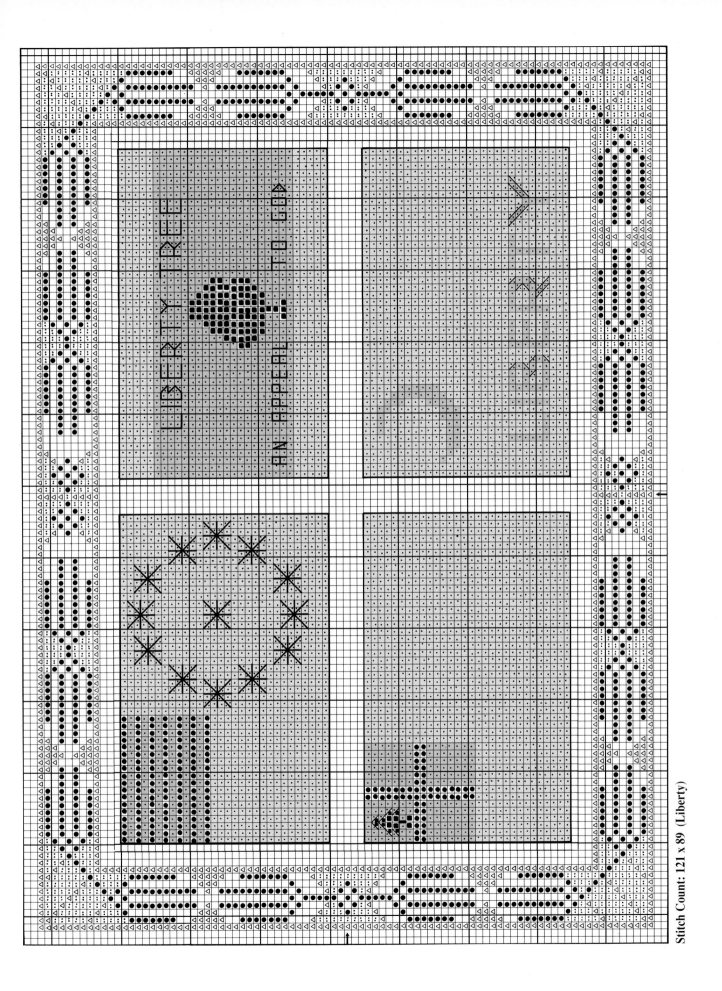

Stitch Count: 121 x 89 (Liberty)

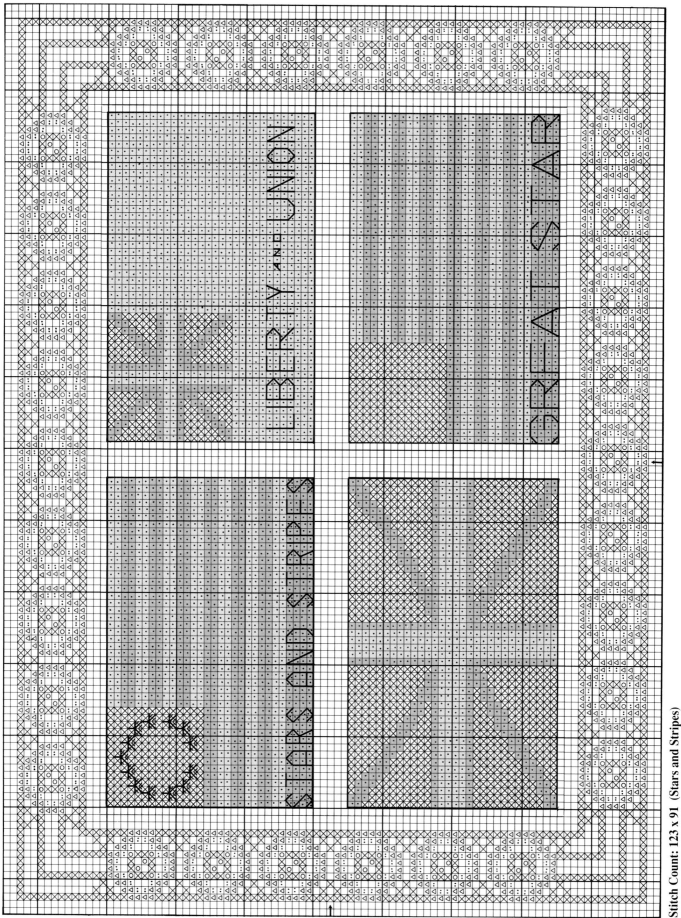

Stitch Count: 123 x 91 (Stars and Stripes)

Stitch Count: 123 x 91 (Confederate)

# Bewitching Windsock

## SAMPLE

Stitched on Waste Canvas 10, the finished design size is 5⅛" x 7⅝". The canvas was cut 7" x 10". The fabric was cut 15" x 22".

| FABRICS | DESIGN SIZES |
|---------|--------------|
| Aida 11 | 4⅝" x 6⅞" |
| Aida 14 | 3⅝" x 5½" |
| Aida 18 | 2⅞" x 4¼" |
| Hardanger 22 | 2⅜" x 3½" |

## MATERIALS

Completed cross-stitch on green waterproof rip-stop fabric; matching thread
1½ yards of black waterproof rip-stop fabric; matching thread
⅝ yard (1"-wide) belting
5 yards (⅛"-wide) black satin ribbon
White dressmaker's pencil

## DIRECTIONS

All seam allowances are ½".

**1.** With design centered, trim design piece to 14" x 21½". From black fabric, cut 1 (17¼" x 21½") piece for hat; cut 1 (6" x 43") strip for hat ruffle; cut 1 (11" x 43") strip for collar ruffle; and cut 11 (2¾" x 30") strips for streamers.

**2.** With right sides facing, stitch the 14" edges of design piece together to make a tube. Trim seam to ¼". Repeat with hat piece, stitching the 17¼" edges together. Finish top edge of hat by folding ¼" to wrong side and stitching.

**3.** Overlap ends of belting 1" and stitch together. Place belting on wrong side at top of hat. Fold top hemmed edge of hat over belting. Stitch hemmed edge to hat, making a 1½" casing.

**4.** To make hat ruffle, with wrong sides facing, fold 6" x 43" strip in half lengthwise. Stitch ends together to make a circle. Stitch 2 rows of gathering stitches, ¼" apart, around long raw edge of ruffle. Gather ruffle to fit hat bottom. With raw edges aligned and ruffle seam aligned with center back hat seam, stitch ruffle to right side of hat bottom.

**5.** With right sides facing, raw edges and seams aligned, and ruffle sandwiched between, stitch top of green tube to bottom of hat, sewing on ruffle stitching line. Stitch again, ¼" from edge.

**6.** To make collar ruffle, follow instructions in Step 4 to gather 11" x 43" strip and attach to green tube bottom.

**7.** To make streamers, cut 1 end of each 2¾" x 30" strip to a point. Finish long edges and points by turning under ¼" and stitching a narrow hem. With raw edges aligned, pin straight edge of streamers over collar ruffle, overlapping ¼" on each side and adjusting as needed to fit around bottom edge of green tube. Stitch streamers to tube, sewing on ruffle stitching line. Stitch again, ¼" from edge.

**8.** For hanger, with white pencil, mark 4 points (2 on front, 2 on back), about 3½" in from each side on wrong side at top of hat, just above stitching line of casing. Cut 4 (45") lengths of ribbon. Machine-tack 1 end of 1 ribbon securely to each mark. Knot free ends together.

| Anchor | | DMC (used for sample) | |
|--------|--|----------------------|--|
| **Step 1:** Cross-stitch (6 strands) | | | |
| 306 | | 725 | Topaz |
| 307 | | 977 | Golden Brown-lt. |
| 308 | | 976 | Golden Brown-med. |
| 355 | | 975 | Golden Brown-dk. |
| 349 | | 921 | Copper |
| 874 | | 834 | Olive Green-vy. lt. |
| 889 | | 831 | Olive Green-med. |
| 906 | | 829 | Olive Green-vy. dk. |
| 862 | | 520 | Fern Green-dk. |
| 370 | | 434 | Brown-lt. |
| 8581 | | 3023 | Brown Gray-lt. |
| 403 | | 310 | Black |
| **Step 2:** Backstitch (2 strands) | | | |
| 403 | | 310 | Black |

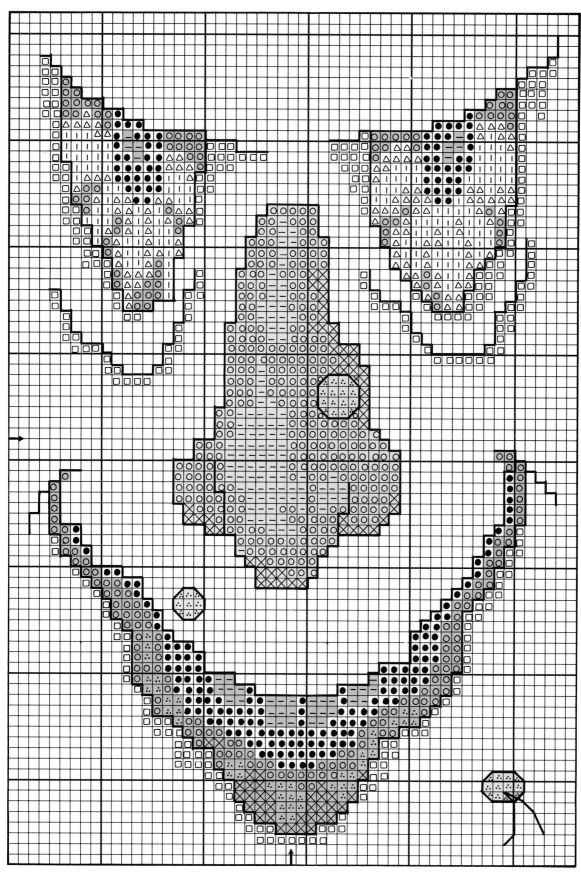

**Stitch Count: 51 x 76**

# Kris Kringle

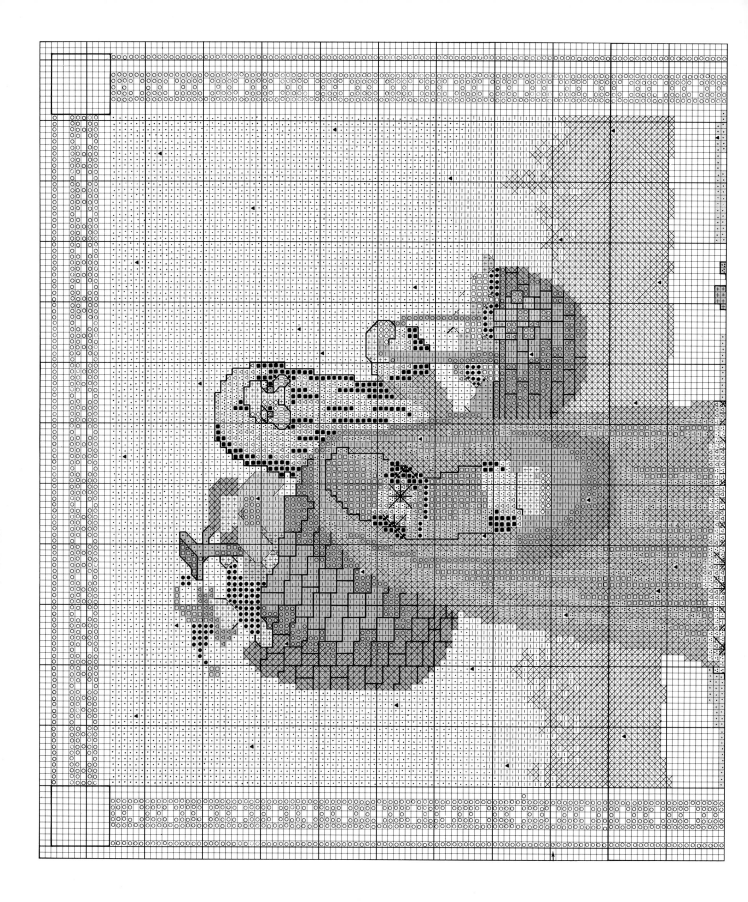

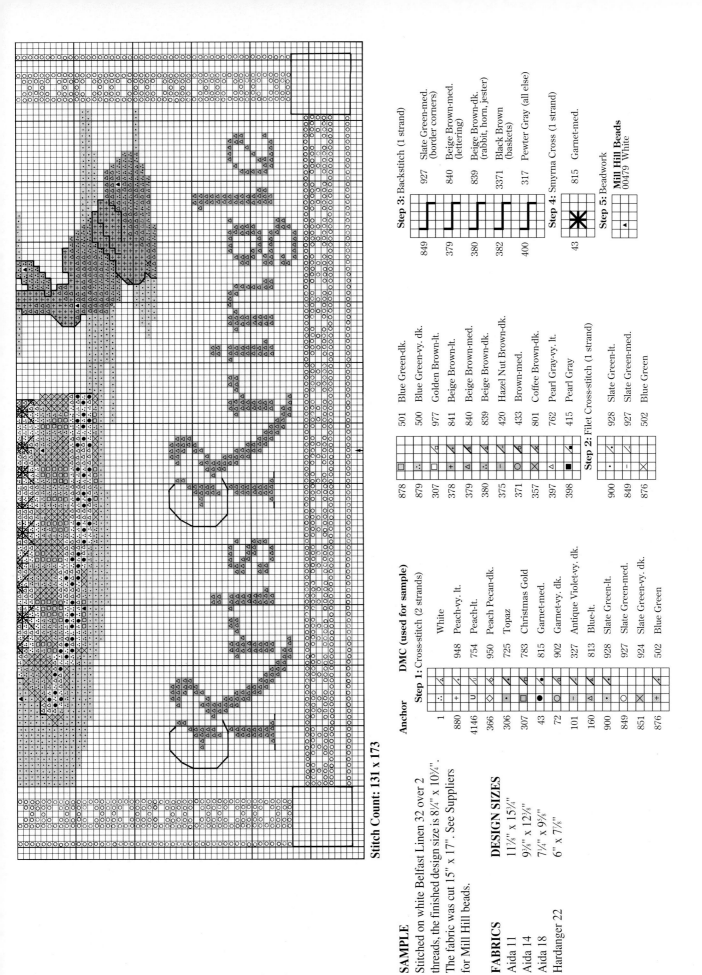

**Stitch Count: 131 x 173**

## SAMPLE

Stitched on white Belfast Linen 32 over 2 threads, the finished design size is 8¼" x 10¾". The fabric was cut 15" x 17". See Suppliers for Mill Hill beads.

| FABRICS | DESIGN SIZES |
|---|---|
| Aida 11 | 11⅞" x 15¾" |
| Aida 14 | 9⅜" x 12⅜" |
| Aida 18 | 7¼" x 9⅞" |
| Hardanger 22 | 6" x 7⅞" |

**Anchor** | **DMC (used for sample)**

**Step 1:** Cross-stitch (2 strands)

| | Anchor | DMC | |
|---|---|---|---|
| | 1 | | White |
| | 880 | 948 | Peach-vy. lt. |
| | 4146 | 754 | Peach-lt. |
| | 366 | 950 | Peach Pecan-dk. |
| | 306 | 725 | Topaz |
| | 307 | 783 | Christmas Gold |
| | 43 | 815 | Garnet-med. |
| | 72 | 902 | Garnet-vy. dk. |
| | 101 | 327 | Antique Violet-vy. dk. |
| | 160 | 813 | Blue-lt. |
| | 900 | 928 | Slate Green-lt. |
| | 849 | 927 | Slate Green-med. |
| | 851 | 924 | Slate Green-vy. dk. |
| | 876 | 502 | Blue Green |

| | Anchor | DMC | |
|---|---|---|---|
| | 878 | 501 | Blue Green-dk. |
| | 879 | 500 | Blue Green-vy. dk. |
| | 307 | 977 | Golden Brown-lt. |
| | 378 | 841 | Beige Brown-lt. |
| | 379 | 840 | Beige Brown-med. |
| | 380 | 839 | Beige Brown-dk. |
| | 375 | 420 | Hazel Nut Brown-dk. |
| | 371 | 433 | Brown-med. |
| | 357 | 801 | Coffee Brown-dk. |
| | 397 | 762 | Pearl Gray-vy. lt. |
| | 398 | 415 | Pearl Gray |

**Step 2:** Filet Cross-stitch (1 strand)

| | Anchor | DMC | |
|---|---|---|---|
| | 900 | 928 | Slate Green-lt. |
| | 849 | 927 | Slate Green-med. |
| | 876 | 502 | Blue Green |

**Step 3:** Backstitch (1 strand)

| | Anchor | DMC | |
|---|---|---|---|
| | 849 | 927 | Slate Green-med. (border corners) |
| | 379 | 840 | Beige Brown-med. (lettering) |
| | 380 | 839 | Beige Brown-dk. (rabbit, horn, jester) |
| | 382 | 3371 | Black Brown (baskets) |
| | 400 | 317 | Pewter Gray (all else) |

**Step 4:** Smyrna Cross (1 strand)

| | Anchor | DMC | |
|---|---|---|---|
| | 43 | 815 | Garnet-med. |

**Step 5:** Beadwork

**Mill Hill Beads**
00479 White

# *Père Noël*

**SAMPLE**
Stitched on white Belfast Linen 32 over 2 threads, the finished design size is 8¼" x 10¾". The fabric was cut 15" x 17".

| FABRICS | DESIGN SIZES |
|---|---|
| Aida 11 | 11⅞" x 15¾" |
| Aida 14 | 9⅜" x 12⅜" |
| Aida 18 | 7¼" x 9⅝" |
| Hardanger 22 | 6" x 7⅞" |

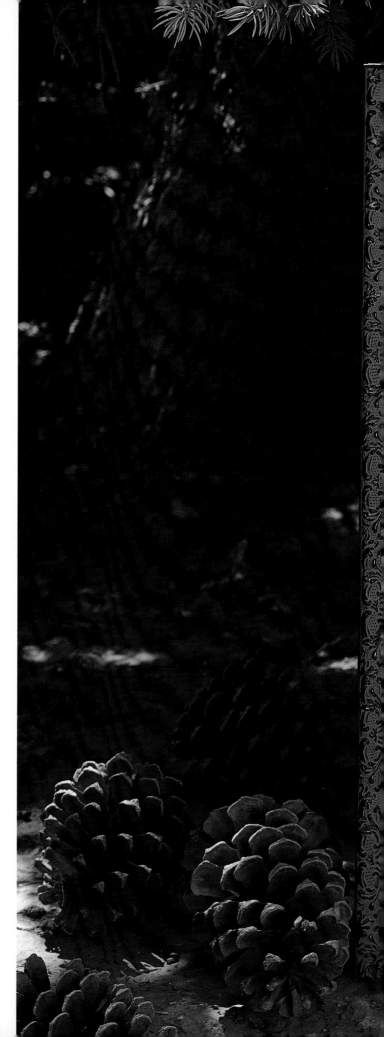

Père Noel

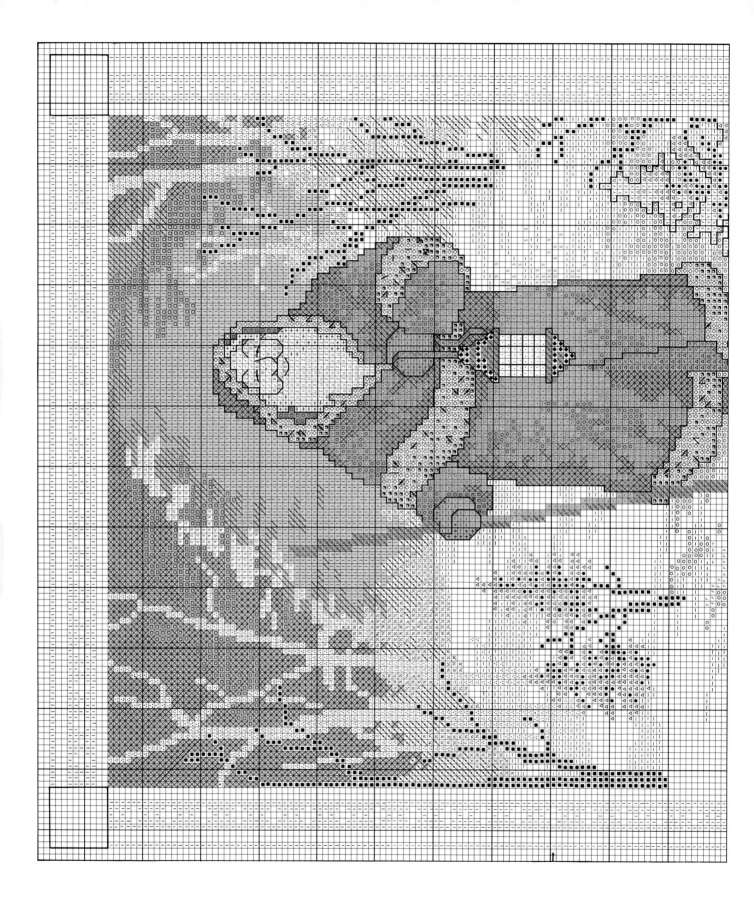

116

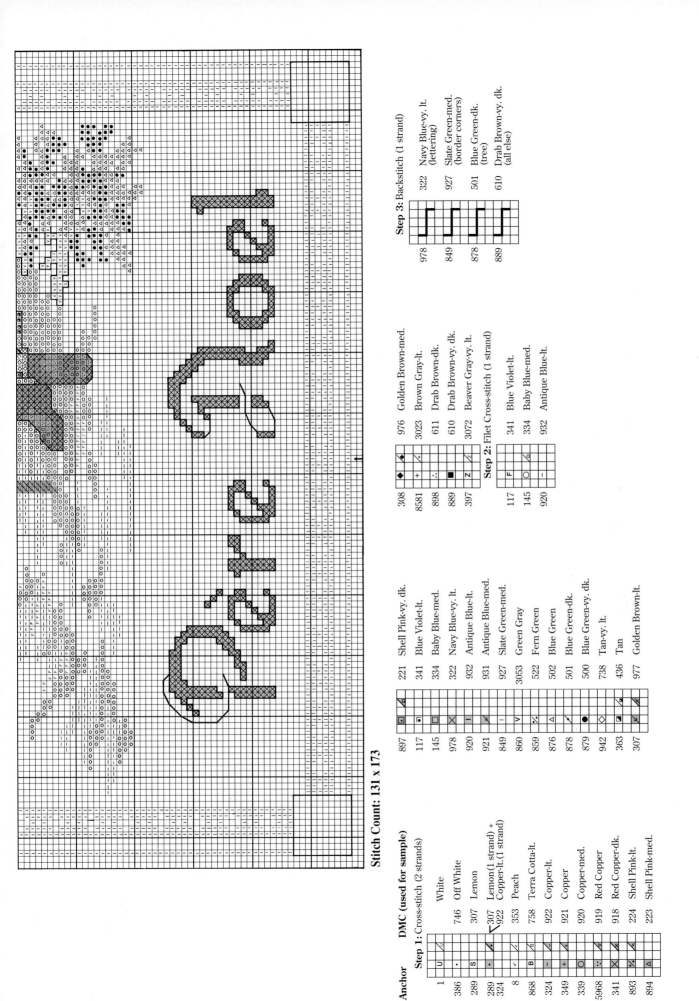

**Stitch Count: 131 x 173**

117

# Father Ice

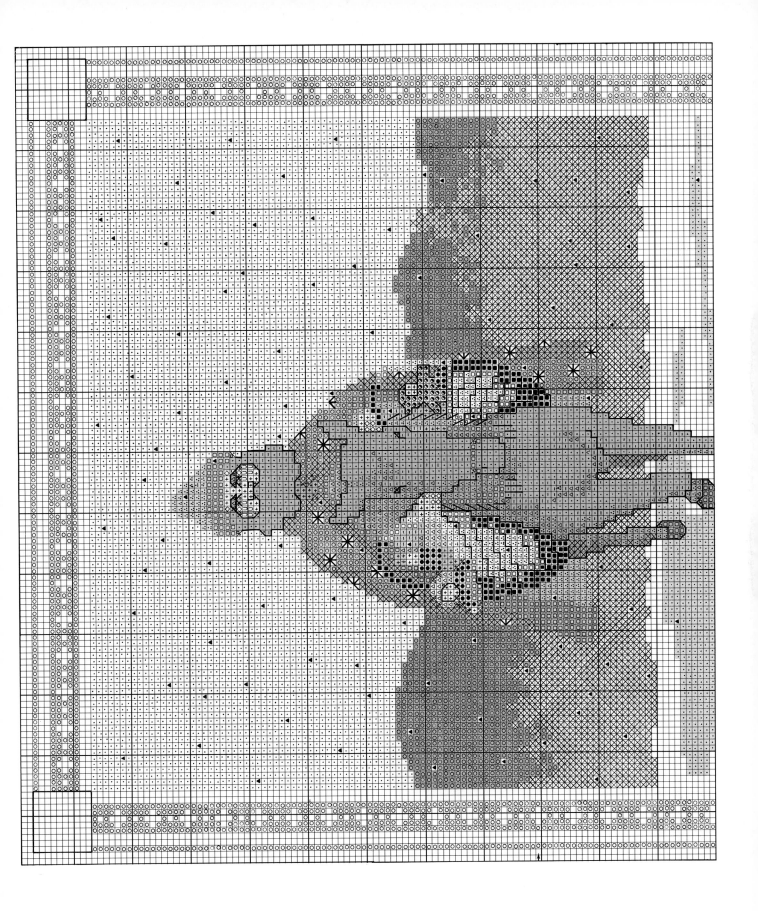

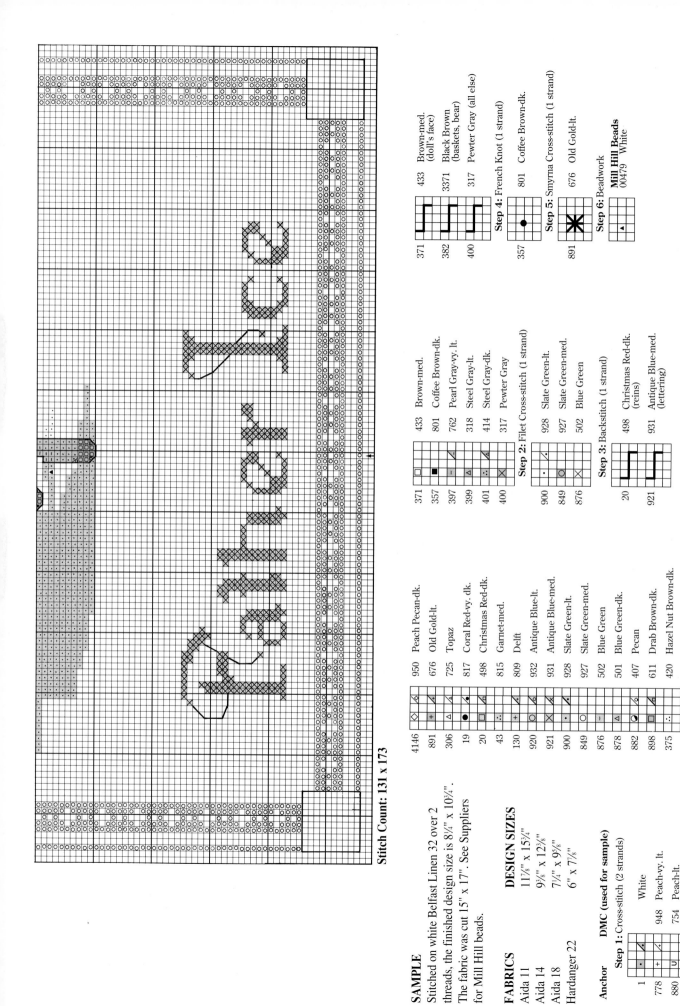

**Stitch Count: 131 x 173**

## SAMPLE

Stitched on white Belfast Linen 32 over 2 threads, the finished design size is 8¼" x 10¾". The fabric was cut 15" x 17". See Suppliers for Mill Hill beads.

## FABRICS / DESIGN SIZES

| FABRICS | DESIGN SIZES |
|---|---|
| Aida 11 | 11⅛" x 15¾" |
| Aida 14 | 9⅛" x 12⅜" |
| Aida 18 | 7¼" x 9⅝" |
| Hardanger 22 | 6" x 7⅞" |

**Anchor    DMC (used for sample)**

**Step 1:** Cross-stitch (2 strands)

| Anchor | DMC | |
|---|---|---|
| 1 | | White |
| 778 | 948 | Peach-vy. lt. |
| 880 | 754 | Peach-lt. |

| Anchor | DMC | |
|---|---|---|
| 4146 | 950 | Peach Pecan-dk. |
| 891 | 676 | Old Gold-lt. |
| 306 | 725 | Topaz |
| 19 | 817 | Coral Red-vy. dk. |
| 20 | 498 | Christmas Red-dk. |
| 43 | 815 | Garnet-med. |
| 130 | 809 | Delft |
| 920 | 932 | Antique Blue-lt. |
| 921 | 931 | Antique Blue-med. |
| 900 | 928 | Slate Green-lt. |
| 849 | 927 | Slate Green-med. |
| 876 | 502 | Blue Green |
| 878 | 501 | Blue Green-dk. |
| 882 | 407 | Pecan |
| 898 | 611 | Drab Brown-dk. |
| 375 | 420 | Hazel Nut Brown-dk. |

| Anchor | DMC | |
|---|---|---|
| 371 | 433 | Brown-med. |
| 357 | 801 | Coffee Brown-dk. |
| 397 | 762 | Pearl Gray-vy. lt. |
| 399 | 318 | Steel Gray-lt. |
| 401 | 414 | Steel Gray-dk. |
| 400 | 317 | Pewter Gray |

**Step 2:** Filet Cross-stitch (1 strand)

| Anchor | DMC | |
|---|---|---|
| 900 | 928 | Slate Green-lt. |
| 849 | 927 | Slate Green-med. |
| 876 | 502 | Blue Green |

**Step 3:** Backstitch (1 strand)

| Anchor | DMC | |
|---|---|---|
| 20 | 498 | Christmas Red-dk. (reins) |
| 921 | 931 | Antique Blue-med. (lettering) |

| Anchor | DMC | |
|---|---|---|
| 371 | 433 | Brown-med. (doll's face) |
| 382 | 3371 | Black Brown (baskets, bear) |
| 400 | 317 | Pewter Gray (all else) |

**Step 4:** French Knot (1 strand)

| Anchor | DMC | |
|---|---|---|
| 357 | 801 | Coffee Brown-dk. |

**Step 5:** Smyrna Cross-stitch (1 strand)

| Anchor | DMC | |
|---|---|---|
| 891 | 676 | Old Gold-lt. |

**Step 6:** Beadwork

**Mill Hill Beads**
00479   White

# St. Nicholas

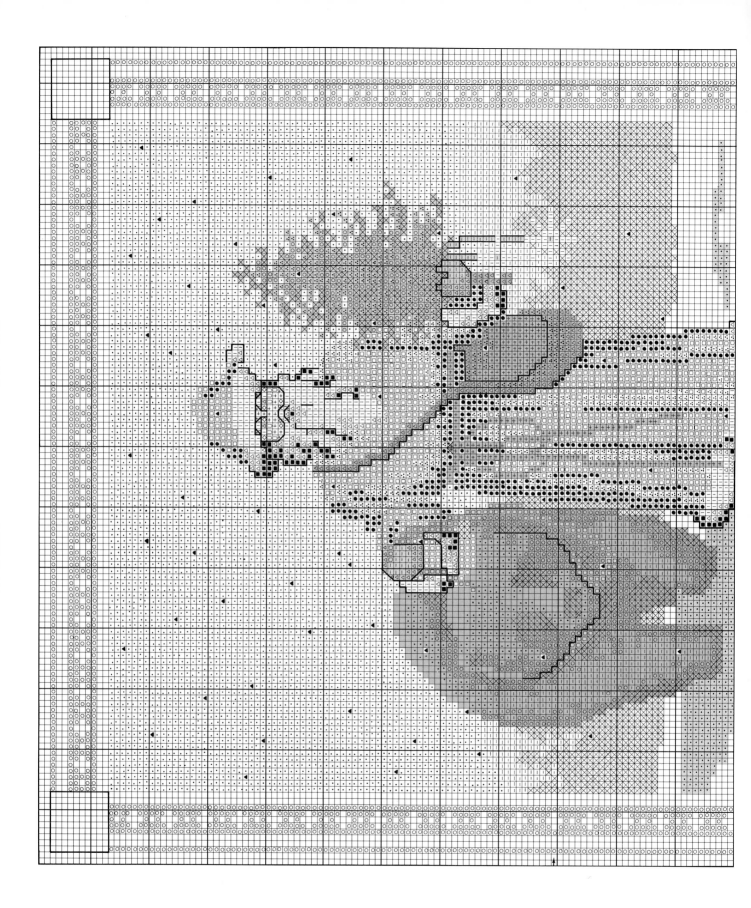

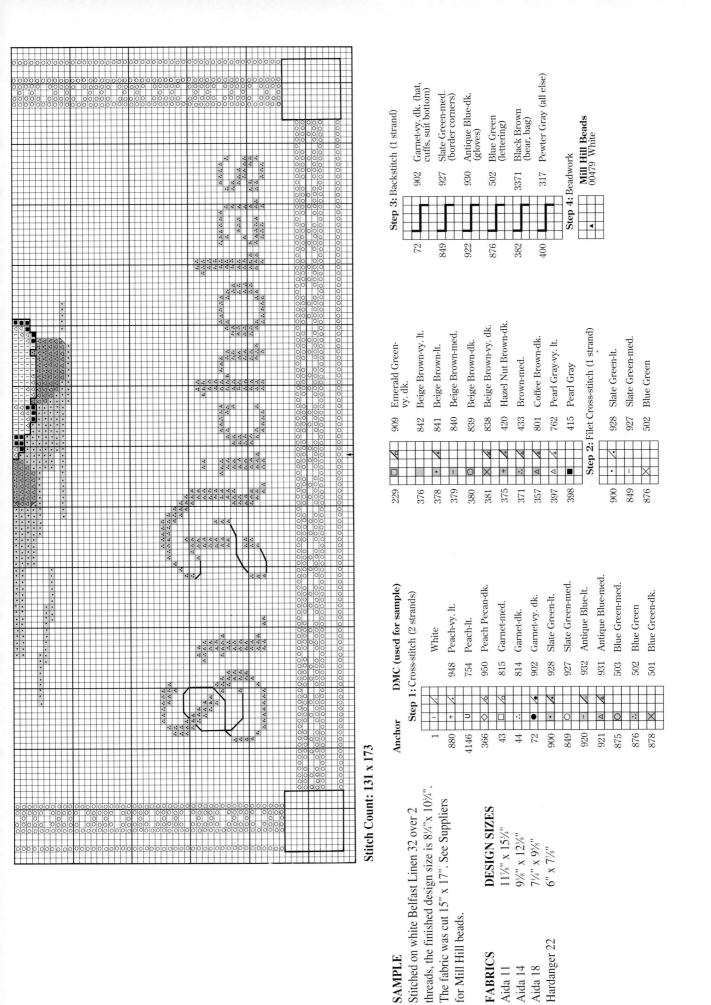

**Stitch Count: 131 x 173**

**SAMPLE**

Stitched on white Belfast Linen 32 over 2 threads, the finished design size is 8¼" x 10¾". The fabric was cut 15" x 17". See Suppliers for Mill Hill beads.

| **FABRICS** | **DESIGN SIZES** |
|---|---|
| Aida 11 | 11⅞" x 15¾" |
| Aida 14 | 9⅜" x 12⅜" |
| Aida 18 | 7¼" x 9⅝" |
| Hardanger 22 | 6" x 7⅞" |

**Anchor**   **DMC (used for sample)**

**Step 1: Cross-stitch (2 strands)**

| | | Anchor | DMC | |
|---|---|---|---|---|
| ⊠ | ⁄ | 1 | | White |
| + | | 880 | 948 | Peach-vy. lt. |
| ⊔ | ⁄ | 4146 | 754 | Peach-lt. |
| ◇ | ⊠ | 366 | 950 | Peach Pecan-dk. |
| □ | ⁄ | 43 | 815 | Garnet-med. |
| ∴ | | 44 | 814 | Garnet-dk. |
| ● | ◐ | 72 | 902 | Garnet-vy. dk. |
| ○ | ⊿ | 900 | 928 | Slate Green-lt. |
| ○ | | 849 | 927 | Slate Green-med. |
| − | ⁄ | 920 | 932 | Antique Blue-lt. |
| ⊿ | ⊿ | 921 | 931 | Antique Blue-med. |
| ∴ | | 875 | 503 | Blue Green-med. |
| ∴ | | 876 | 502 | Blue Green |
| ⊠ | | 878 | 501 | Blue Green-dk. |

| | | Anchor | DMC | |
|---|---|---|---|---|
| □ | ◺ | 229 | 909 | Emerald Green-vy. dk. |
| ▦ | | 376 | 842 | Beige Brown-vy. lt. |
| · | | 378 | 841 | Beige Brown-lt. |
| − | | 379 | 840 | Beige Brown-med. |
| ○ | | 380 | 839 | Beige Brown-dk. |
| ⊠ | | 381 | 838 | Beige Brown-vy. dk. |
| + | | 375 | 420 | Hazel Nut Brown-dk. |
| ∴ | | 371 | 433 | Brown-med. |
| ▲ | | 357 | 801 | Coffee Brown-dk. |
| ▵ | ◿ | 397 | 762 | Pearl Gray-vy. lt. |
| ■ | | 398 | 415 | Pearl Gray |

**Step 2: Filet Cross-stitch (1 strand)**

| | | Anchor | DMC | |
|---|---|---|---|---|
| · | ⁄ | 900 | 928 | Slate Green-lt. |
| − | | 849 | 927 | Slate Green-med. |
| ⊠ | | 876 | 502 | Blue Green |

**Step 3: Backstitch (1 strand)**

| | Anchor | DMC | |
|---|---|---|---|
| | 72 | 902 | Garnet-vy. dk. (hat, cuffs, suit bottom) |
| | 849 | 927 | Slate Green-med. (border corners) |
| | 922 | 930 | Antique Blue-dk. (gloves) |
| | 876 | 502 | Blue Green (lettering) |
| | 382 | 3371 | Black Brown (bear, bag) |
| | 400 | 317 | Pewter Gray (all else) |

**Step 4: Beadwork**

| | **Mill Hill Beads** |
|---|---|
| ▲ | 00479 White |

# Kanaka Loka

**SAMPLE**

Stitched on white Belfast Linen 32 over 2 threads, the finished
design size is 8¼" x 10¾". The fabric was cut 15" x 17".

| FABRICS | DESIGN SIZES |
|---|---|
| Aida 11 | 11⅞" x 15¾" |
| Aida 14 | 9⅜" x 12⅜" |
| Aida 18 | 7¼" x 9⅝" |
| Hardanger 22 | 6" x 7⅞" |

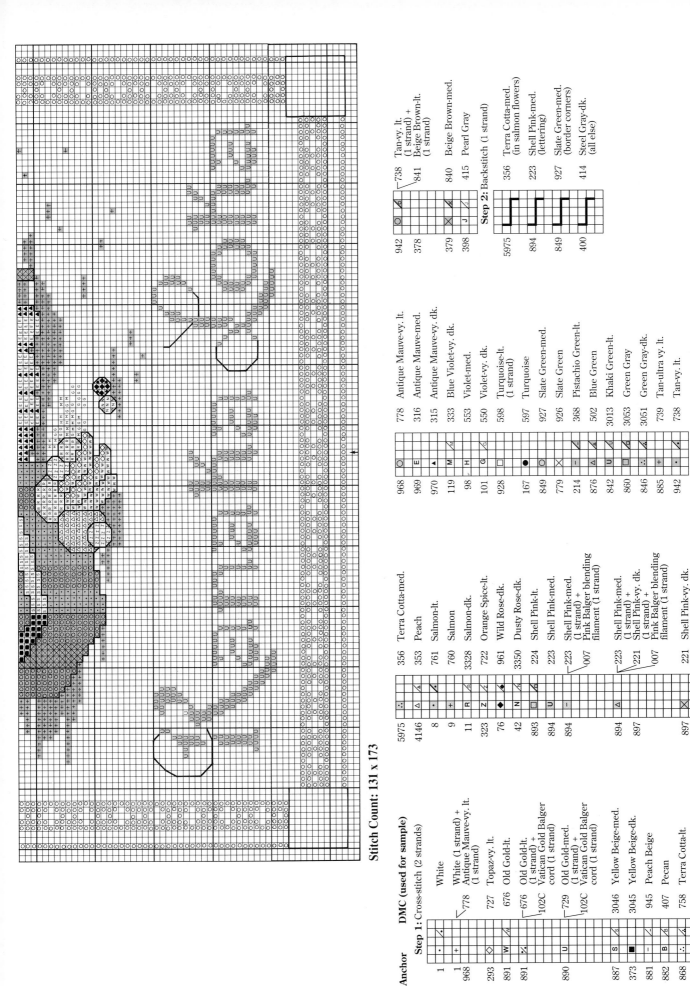

**Stitch Count: 131 x 173**

**Anchor   DMC (used for sample)**

**Step 1: Cross-stitch (2 strands)**

| Anchor | DMC | Color |
|---|---|---|
| 1 | | White |
| 1 | ⌐778 | White (1 strand) + Antique Mauve-vy. lt. (1 strand) |
| 968 | | |
| 293 | 727 | Topaz-vy. lt. |
| 891 | 676 | Old Gold-lt. |
| 891 | ⌐676 102C | Old Gold-lt. (1 strand) + Vatican Gold Balger cord (1 strand) |
| 890 | ⌐729 102C | Old Gold-med. (1 strand) + Vatican Gold Balger cord (1 strand) |
| 887 | 3046 | Yellow Beige-med. |
| 373 | 3045 | Yellow Beige-dk. |
| 881 | 945 | Peach Beige |
| 882 | 407 | Pecan |
| 868 | 758 | Terra Cotta-lt. |

| Anchor | DMC | Color |
|---|---|---|
| 5975 | 356 | Terra Cotta-med. |
| 4146 | 353 | Peach |
| 8 | 761 | Salmon-lt. |
| 9 | 760 | Salmon |
| 11 | 3328 | Salmon-dk. |
| 323 | 722 | Orange Spice-lt. |
| 76 | 961 | Wild Rose-dk. |
| 42 | 3350 | Dusty Rose-dk. |
| 893 | 224 | Shell Pink-lt. |
| 894 | 223 | Shell Pink-med. |
| 894 | ⌐223 007 | Shell Pink-med. (1 strand) + Pink Balger blending filament (1 strand) |
| 894 | ⌐223 221 | Shell Pink-med. (1 strand) + |
| 897 | 221 | Shell Pink-vy. dk. (1 strand) + |
| 897 | 007 | Pink Balger blending filament (1 strand) |
| 897 | 221 | Shell Pink-vy. dk. |

| Anchor | DMC | Color |
|---|---|---|
| 968 | 778 | Antique Mauve-vy. lt. |
| 969 | 316 | Antique Mauve-med. |
| 970 | 315 | Antique Mauve-vy. dk. |
| 119 | 333 | Blue Violet-vy. dk. |
| 98 | 553 | Violet-med. |
| 101 | 550 | Violet-vy. dk. |
| 928 | 598 | Turquoise-lt. (1 strand) |
| 167 | 597 | Turquoise |
| 849 | 927 | Slate Green-med. |
| 779 | 926 | Slate Green |
| 214 | 368 | Pistachio Green-lt. |
| 876 | 502 | Blue Green |
| 842 | 3013 | Khaki Green-lt. |
| 860 | 3053 | Green Gray |
| 846 | 3051 | Green Gray-dk. |
| 885 | 739 | Tan-ultra vy. lt. |
| 942 | 738 | Tan-vy. lt. |

| Anchor | DMC | Color |
|---|---|---|
| 942 | ⌐738 841 | Tan-vy. lt. (1 strand) + Beige Brown-lt. (1 strand) |
| 378 | 840 | Beige Brown-med. |
| 379 | 415 | Pearl Gray |
| 398 | | |

**Step 2: Backstitch (1 strand)**

| Anchor | DMC | Color |
|---|---|---|
| 5975 | 356 | Terra Cotta-med. (in salmon flowers) |
| 894 | 223 | Shell Pink-med. (lettering) |
| 849 | 927 | Slate Green-med. (border corners) |
| 400 | 414 | Steel Gray-dk. (all else) |

# Father Frost

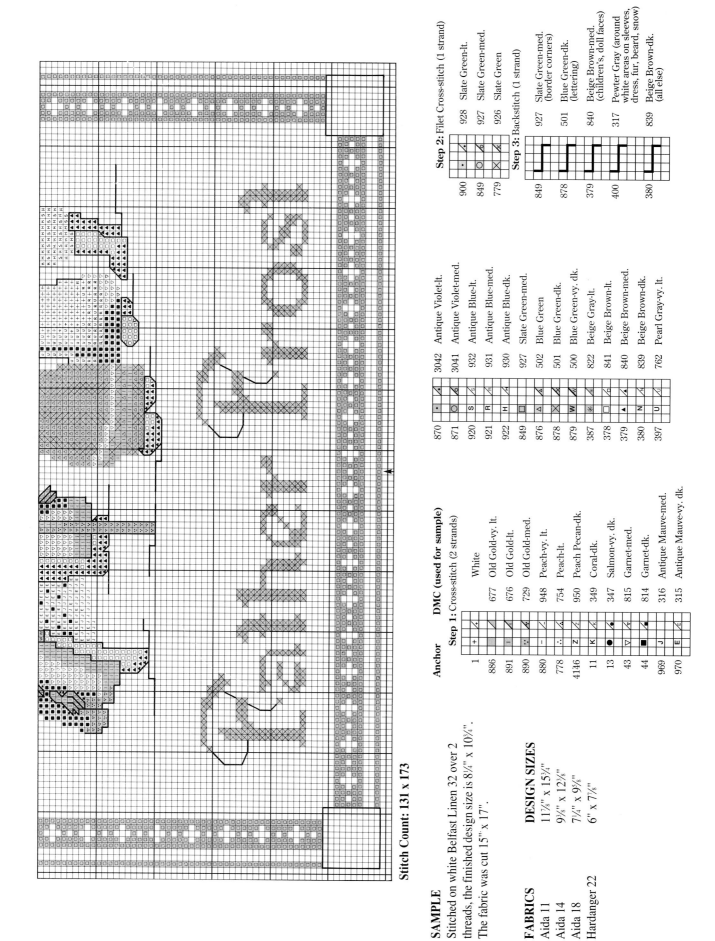

**Stitch Count: 131 x 173**

**SAMPLE**

Stitched on white Belfast Linen 32 over 2 threads, the finished design size is 8¼" x 10¾". The fabric was cut 15" x 17".

**FABRICS**          **DESIGN SIZES**

Aida 11          11⅛" x 15¾"

Aida 14          9⅜" x 12⅜"

Aida 18          7¼" x 9⅝"

Hardanger 22          6" x 7⅞"

| Anchor | DMC (used for sample) |
|---|---|
| **Step 1:** Cross-stitch (2 strands) | |
| 1 | White |
| 886 | 677 Old Gold-vy. lt. |
| 891 | 676 Old Gold-lt. |
| 890 | 729 Old Gold-med. |
| 880 | 948 Peach-vy. lt. |
| 778 | 754 Peach-lt. |
| 4146 | 950 Peach Pecan-dk. |
| 11 | 349 Coral-dk. |
| 13 | 347 Salmon-vy. dk. |
| 43 | 815 Garnet-med. |
| 44 | 814 Garnet-dk. |
| 969 | 316 Antique Mauve-med. |
| 970 | 315 Antique Mauve-vy. dk. |
| 870 | 3042 Antique Violet-lt. |
| 871 | 3041 Antique Violet-med. |
| 920 | 932 Antique Blue-lt. |
| 921 | 931 Antique Blue-med. |
| 922 | 930 Antique Blue-dk. |
| 849 | 927 Slate Green-med. |
| 876 | 502 Blue Green |
| 878 | 501 Blue Green-dk. |
| 879 | 500 Blue Green-vy. dk. |
| 387 | 822 Beige Gray-lt. |
| 378 | 841 Beige Brown-lt. |
| 379 | 840 Beige Brown-med. |
| 380 | 839 Beige Brown-dk. |
| 397 | 762 Pearl Gray-vy. lt. |

| | | |
|---|---|---|
| **Step 2:** Filet Cross-stitch (1 strand) | | |
| 900 | 928 | Slate Green-lt. |
| 849 | 927 | Slate Green-med. |
| 779 | 926 | Slate Green |

| | | |
|---|---|---|
| **Step 3:** Backstitch (1 strand) | | |
| 849 | 927 | Slate Green-med. (border corners) |
| 878 | 501 | Blue Green-dk. (lettering) |
| 379 | 840 | Beige Brown-med. (children's, doll faces) |
| 400 | 317 | Pewter Gray (around white areas on sleeves, dress, fur, beard, snow) |
| 380 | 839 | Beige Brown-dk. (all else) |

# Sinter Klaas

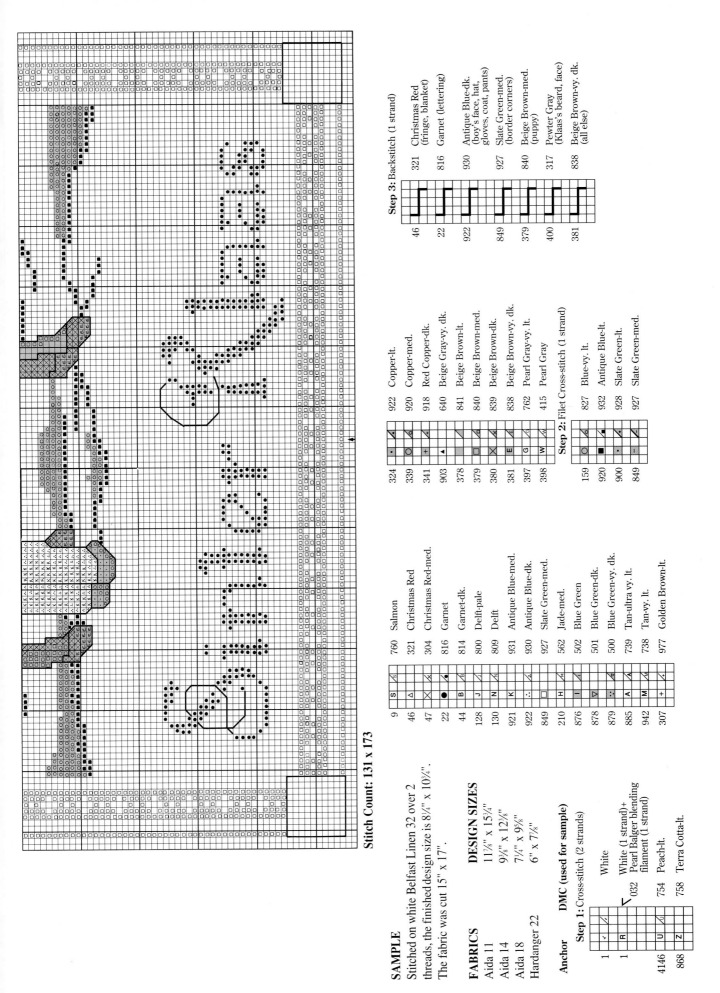

**Stitch Count: 131 x 173**

## SAMPLE

Stitched on white Belfast Linen 32 over 2 threads, the finished design size is 8¼" x 10¾". The fabric was cut 15" x 17".

| FABRICS | DESIGN SIZES |
|---|---|
| Aida 11 | 11⅞" x 15¾" |
| Aida 14 | 9⅜" x 12⅜" |
| Aida 18 | 7¼" x 9⅝" |
| Hardanger 22 | 6" x 7⅞" |

**Step 1:** Cross-stitch (2 strands)

| Anchor | | DMC (used for sample) |
|---|---|---|
| 1 | | White |
| 1 | R | White (1 strand)+ 032 Pearl Balger blending filament (1 strand) |
| 4146 | | 754 Peach-lt. |
| 868 | | 758 Terra Cotta-lt. |

| Anchor | | DMC | |
|---|---|---|---|
| 9 | S | 760 | Salmon |
| 46 | | 321 | Christmas Red |
| 47 | | 304 | Christmas Red-med. |
| 22 | | 816 | Garnet |
| 44 | B | 814 | Garnet-dk. |
| 128 | J | 800 | Delft-pale |
| 130 | N | 809 | Delft |
| 921 | K | 931 | Antique Blue-med. |
| 922 | | 930 | Antique Blue-dk. |
| 849 | | 927 | Slate Green-med. |
| 210 | H | 562 | Jade-med. |
| 876 | I | 502 | Blue Green |
| 878 | | 501 | Blue Green-dk. |
| 879 | | 500 | Blue Green-vy. dk. |
| 885 | A | 739 | Tan-ultra vy. lt. |
| 942 | M | 738 | Tan-vy. lt. |
| 307 | + | 977 | Golden Brown-lt. |

| Anchor | | DMC | |
|---|---|---|---|
| 324 | • | 922 | Copper-lt. |
| 339 | O | 920 | Copper-med. |
| 341 | + | 918 | Red Copper-dk. |
| 903 | ▲ | 640 | Beige Gray-vy. dk. |
| 378 | | 841 | Beige Brown-lt. |
| 379 | | 840 | Beige Brown-med. |
| 380 | X | 839 | Beige Brown-dk. |
| 381 | E | 838 | Beige Brown-vy. dk. |
| 397 | G | 762 | Pearl Gray-vy. lt. |
| 398 | W | 415 | Pearl Gray |

**Step 2:** Filet Cross-stitch (1 strand)

| Anchor | | DMC | |
|---|---|---|---|
| 159 | O | 827 | Blue-vy. lt. |
| 920 | ■ | 932 | Antique Blue-lt. |
| 900 | ▷ | 928 | Slate Green-lt. |
| 849 | – | 927 | Slate Green-med. |

**Step 3:** Backstitch (1 strand)

| Anchor | DMC | |
|---|---|---|
| 46 | 321 | Christmas Red (fringe, blanket) |
| 22 | 816 | Garnet (lettering) |
| 922 | 930 | Antique Blue-dk. (boy's face, hat, gloves, coat, pants) |
| 849 | 927 | Slate Green-med. (border corners) |
| 379 | 840 | Beige Brown-med. (puppy) |
| 400 | 317 | Pewter Gray (Klaas's beard, face) |
| 381 | 838 | Beige Brown-vy. dk. (all else) |

# New Creations

Our final chapter introduces brand-new creations from The Vanessa-Ann Collection. You'll find soft florals and geometric shapes that work together to form a delicate look in Floral Elegance. A Home Sweet Home design will fill your home with a springlike feeling of warmth and welcome. Enjoy a taste of The Great Outdoors anytime with our rustic framed piece that depicts nature's wonders, or keep the doctor away with An Apple a Day.

# An Apple a Day

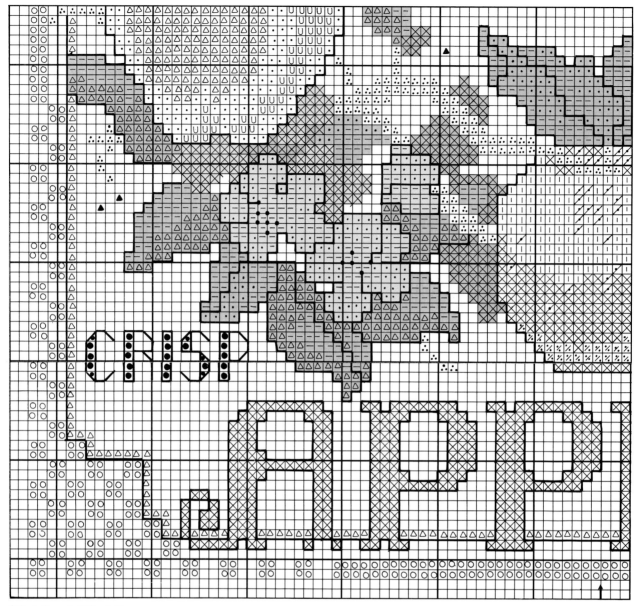

**Stitch Count: 120 x 148**

## SAMPLE

Stitched on cream Belfast Linen 32 over 2 threads, the finished design size is 7½" x 9¼". The fabric was cut 14" x 16".

### FABRICS

Aida 11
Aida 14
Aida 18
Hardanger 22

### DESIGN SIZES

10⅞" x 13½"
8⅝" x 10⅝"
6⅝" x 8¼"
5½" x 6¾"

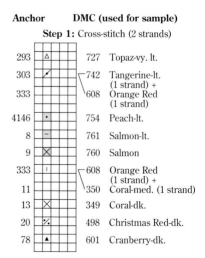

| Anchor | | DMC (used for sample) | |
|---|---|---|---|
| **Step 1:** Cross-stitch (2 strands) | | | |
| 293 | △ | 727 | Topaz-vy. lt. |
| 303 | ╱ | 742 | Tangerine-lt. (1 strand) + |
| 333 | | 608 | Orange Red (1 strand) |
| 4146 | • | 754 | Peach-lt. |
| 8 | − | 761 | Salmon-lt. |
| 9 | ⊠ | 760 | Salmon |
| 333 | I | 608 | Orange Red (1 strand) + |
| 11 | | 350 | Coral-med. (1 strand) |
| 13 | ☒ | 349 | Coral-dk. |
| 20 | ⊠ | 498 | Christmas Red-dk. |
| 78 | ▲ | 601 | Cranberry-dk. |

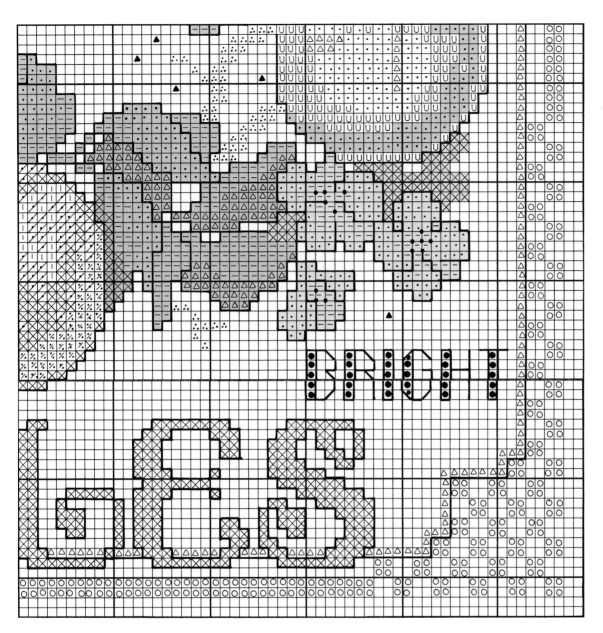

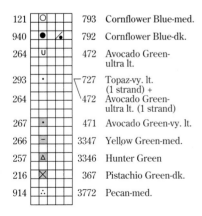

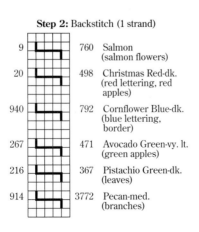

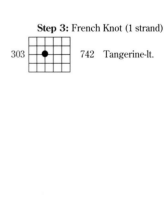

| 121 | ○ | | | | 793 | Cornflower Blue-med. |
| 940 | ● | / | | | 792 | Cornflower Blue-dk. |
| 264 | U | | | | 472 | Avocado Green-<br>ultra lt. |
| 293 | · | | ⌐ | 727 | Topaz-vy. lt.<br>(1 strand) + |
| 264 | | | ⌐ | 472 | Avocado Green-<br>ultra lt. (1 strand) |
| 267 | ▪ | | | | 471 | Avocado Green-vy. lt. |
| 266 | ‒ | | | | 3347 | Yellow Green-med. |
| 257 | △ | | | | 3346 | Hunter Green |
| 216 | ✕ | | | | 367 | Pistachio Green-dk. |
| 914 | ∴ | | | | 3772 | Pecan-med. |

**Step 2:** Backstitch (1 strand)

| 9 | | 760 | Salmon<br>(salmon flowers) |
| 20 | | 498 | Christmas Red-dk.<br>(red lettering, red<br>apples) |
| 940 | | 792 | Cornflower Blue-dk.<br>(blue lettering,<br>border) |
| 267 | | 471 | Avocado Green-vy. lt.<br>(green apples) |
| 216 | | 367 | Pistachio Green-dk.<br>(leaves) |
| 914 | | 3772 | Pecan-med.<br>(branches) |

**Step 3:** French Knot (1 strand)

| 303 | ● | | 742 | Tangerine-lt. |

# Carousel Tiger

**Stitch Count: 113 x 113**

## SAMPLE

Stitched on white Murano 30 over 2 threads, the finished design size is 7½" x 7½". The fabric was cut 14" x 14".

## FABRICS

Aida 11
Aida 14
Aida 18
Hardanger 22

## DESIGN SIZES

10¼" x 10¼"
8½" x 8½"
6¼" x 6¼"
5⅛" x 5⅛"

| Anchor | | DMC (used for sample) | |
|---|---|---|---|

**Step 1: Cross-stitch (2 strands)**

| 886 | · | 677 | Old Gold-vy. lt. |
| 323 | △ ◿ | 722 | Orange Spice-lt. |
| 8 | − | 761 | Salmon-lt. |
| 337 | + | 3778 | Terra Cotta |
| 10 | ⊙ | 3712 | Salmon-med. |
| 13 | ▲ | 347 | Salmon-vy. dk. |
| 66 | ✕ | 3688 | Mauve-med. |
| 69 | ∴ | 3687 | Mauve |
| 42 | − | 3350 | Dusty Rose-dk. |
| 95 | □ | 554 | Violet-lt. |
| 119 | ⊙ | 333 | Blue Violet-vy. dk. |

| 42 | ⊠ | 3350 | Dusty Rose-dk. (1 strand) + |
| 119 | | 333 | Blue Violet-vy. dk. (1 strand) |
| 872 | ∴ | 3740 | Antique Violet-dk. |
| 928 | ∴ | 598 | Turquoise-lt. |
| 203 | + | 564 | Jade-vy. lt. |
| 210 | ■ | 562 | Jade-med. |
| 214 | − | 368 | Pistachio Green-lt. |
| 216 | △ | 367 | Pistachio Green-dk. |
| 397 | · ◿ | 762 | Pearl Gray-vy. lt. |
| 400 | □ | 414 | Steel Gray-dk. |
| 401 | ✕ ◿ | 535 | Ash Gray-vy. lt. |

**Step 2: Filet Cross-stitch (1 strand)**

| 8 | · | 761 | Salmon-lt. |
| 66 | ○ | 3688 | Mauve-med. |
| 928 | □ | 598 | Turquoise-lt. |
| 214 | ● | 368 | Pistachio Green-lt. |

**Step 3: Backstitch (1 strand)**

| 236 | ▬ | 3799 | Pewter Gray-vy. dk. |

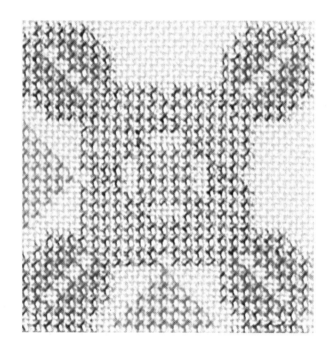

146

# The Great Outdoors

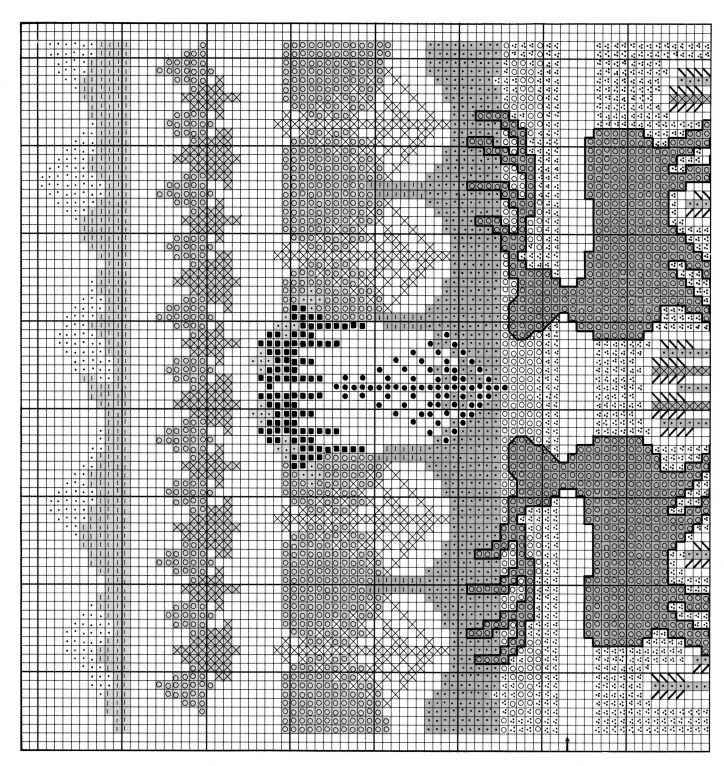

## SAMPLE

Stitched on caramel Annabelle 28 over 2 threads, the finished design size is 5⅝" x 9". The fabric was cut 12" x 15".

| FABRICS | DESIGN SIZES |
|---|---|
| Aida 11 | 7⅛" x 11½" |
| Aida 14 | 5⅝" x 9" |
| Aida 18 | 4⅜" x 7" |
| Hardanger 22 | 3⅝" x 5¾" |

**Anchor**     **DMC (used for sample)**

**Step 1:** Cross-stitch (2 strands)

| Anchor | | | DMC | (used for sample) |
|---|---|---|---|---|
| 926 | · | ⁄ | | Ecru |
| 9 | □ | | 760 | Salmon |
| 10 | ■ | | 3712 | Salmon-med. |
| 920 | − | | 932 | Antique Blue-lt. |
| 921 | · | ⁄ | 931 | Antique Blue-med. |
| 167 | ⌶ | ⁄ | 519 | Sky Blue |
| 168 | ▲ | | 518 | Wedgwood-lt. |
| 875 | △ | ⁄ | 503 | Blue Green-med. |
| 876 | ✕ | | 502 | Blue Green |

148

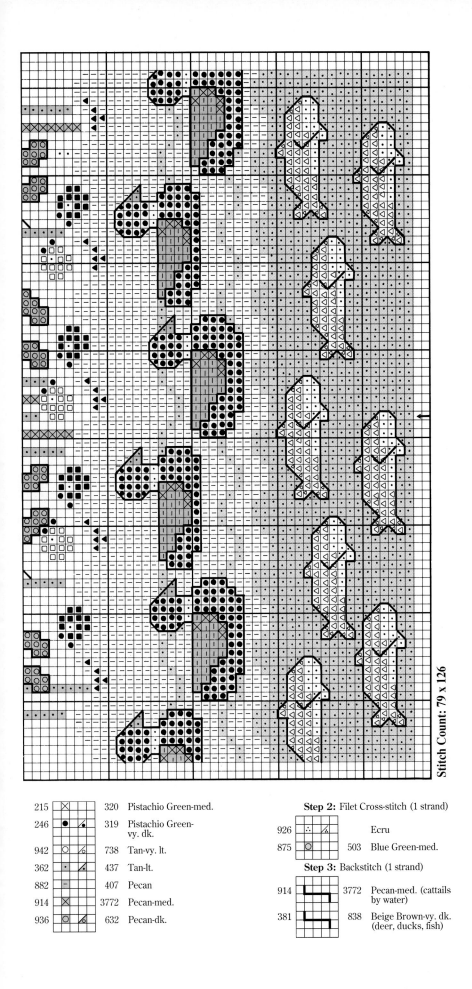

**Stitch Count: 79 x 126**

| 215 | | | 320 | Pistachio Green-med. |
|-----|---|---|-----|----------------------|
| 246 | | | 319 | Pistachio Green-vy. dk. |
| 942 | | | 738 | Tan-vy. lt. |
| 362 | | | 437 | Tan-lt. |
| 882 | | | 407 | Pecan |
| 914 | | | 3772 | Pecan-med. |
| 936 | | | 632 | Pecan-dk. |

**Step 2:** Filet Cross-stitch (1 strand)

| 926 | | | | Ecru |
|-----|---|---|---|------|
| 875 | | | 503 | Blue Green-med. |

**Step 3:** Backstitch (1 strand)

| 914 | | 3772 | Pecan-med. (cattails by water) |
|-----|---|------|--------------------------------|
| 381 | | 838 | Beige Brown-vy. dk. (deer, ducks, fish) |

149

# Floral Elegance

**Stitch Count: 71 x 98**

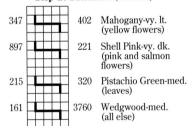

| Anchor | | DMC (used for sample) | |
|---|---|---|---|
| **Step 1:** Cross-stitch (2 strands) | | | |
| 300 | · | 745 | Yellow-lt. pale |
| 297 | □ | 743 | Yellow-med. |
| 347 | ▲ | 402 | Mahogany-vy. lt. |
| 24 | ∴ | 776 | Pink-med. |
| 25 | ◎ | 3326 | Rose-lt. |
| 27 | ⊠ | 899 | Rose-med. |
| 8 | ı | 761 | Salmon-lt. |
| 10 | ∴ | 3712 | Salmon-med. |
| 13 | ✕ | 347 | Salmon-vy. dk. |
| 897 | ● | 221 | Shell Pink-vy. dk. |
| 869 | ◯ | 3743 | Antique Violet-vy. lt. |
| 975 | – | 3753 | Antique Blue-vy. lt. |
| 264 | △ | 772 | Pine Green-lt. |
| 208 | ⊠ | 563 | Jade-lt. |
| 213 | □ | 369 | Pistachio Green-vy. lt. |
| 215 | | 320 | Pistachio Green-med. |
| 900 | | 928 | Slate Green-lt. |
| **Step 2:** Backstitch (1 strand) | | | |
| 347 | | 402 | Mahogany-vy. lt. (yellow flowers) |
| 897 | | 221 | Shell Pink-vy. dk. (pink and salmon flowers) |
| 215 | | 320 | Pistachio Green-med. (leaves) |
| 161 | | 3760 | Wedgwood-med. (all else) |

## SAMPLE

Stitched on white Linda 27 over 2 threads, the finished design size is 5¼" x 7¼". The fabric was cut 12" x 14".

## FABRICS

Aida 11
Aida 14
Aida 18
Hardanger 22

## DESIGN SIZES

6½" x 8⅞"
5⅛" x 7"
4" x 5⅛"
3¼" x 4½"

# Home Sweet Home

**SAMPLE**
Stitched on white Dublin Linen 25 over 2 threads, the finished design size is 16½" x 12¾". The fabric was cut 23" x 19".

| FABRICS | DESIGN SIZES |
|---|---|
| Aida 11 | 18¾" x 14½" |
| Aida 14 | 14¾" x 11⅜" |
| Aida 18 | 11½" x 8⅞" |
| Hardanger 22 | 9⅜" x 7¼" |

**Stitch Count: 206 x 160**

154

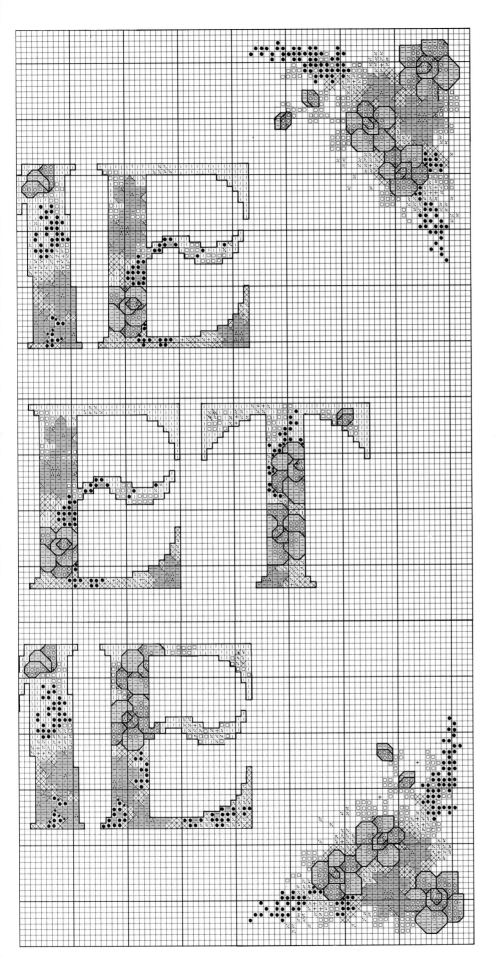

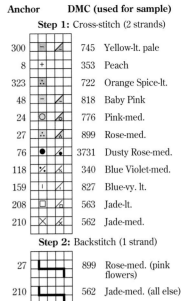

| Anchor | | DMC | (used for sample) |
|---|---|---|---|

**Step 1: Cross-stitch (2 strands)**

| 300 | 745 | Yellow-lt. pale |
|---|---|---|
| 8 | 353 | Peach |
| 323 | 722 | Orange Spice-lt. |
| 48 | 818 | Baby Pink |
| 24 | 776 | Pink-med. |
| 27 | 899 | Rose-med. |
| 76 | 3731 | Dusty Rose-med. |
| 118 | 340 | Blue Violet-med. |
| 159 | 827 | Blue-vy. lt. |
| 208 | 563 | Jade-lt. |
| 210 | 562 | Jade-med. |

**Step 2: Backstitch (1 strand)**

| 27 | 899 | Rose-med. (pink flowers) |
|---|---|---|
| 210 | 562 | Jade-med. (all else) |

...and
they lived
happily
ever after...
DAVID
AND
FRANCES
McMILLAN

AUGUST 25, 1962

# Happily Ever After

**Stitch Count: 68 x 94**

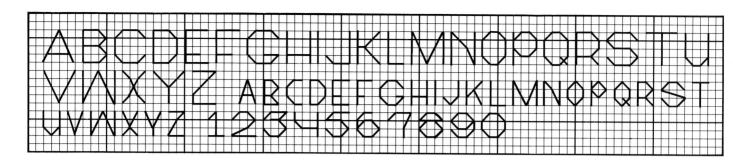

## SAMPLE

Stitched on white Murano 30 over 2 threads, the finished design size is 4½" x 6¼". The fabric was cut 11" x 13". See Suppliers for candle screen.

| FABRICS | DESIGN SIZES |
|---|---|
| Aida 11 | 6⅛" x 8½" |
| Aida 14 | 4⅞" x 6¾" |
| Aida 18 | 3¾" x 5¼" |
| Hardanger 22 | 3⅛" x 4¼" |

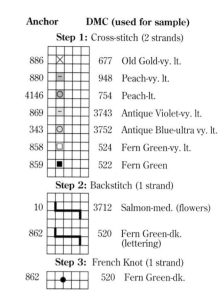

| Anchor | | DMC (used for sample) | |
|---|---|---|---|
| **Step 1:** Cross-stitch (2 strands) | | | |
| 886 | ☒ | 677 | Old Gold-vy. lt. |
| 880 | ⊟ | 948 | Peach-vy. lt. |
| 4146 | ⊙ | 754 | Peach-lt. |
| 869 | ⊟ | 3743 | Antique Violet-vy. lt. |
| 343 | ⊙ | 3752 | Antique Blue-ultra vy. lt. |
| 858 | ☐ | 524 | Fern Green-vy. lt. |
| 859 | ■ | 522 | Fern Green |
| **Step 2:** Backstitch (1 strand) | | | |
| 10 | | 3712 | Salmon-med. (flowers) |
| 862 | | 520 | Fern Green-dk. (lettering) |
| **Step 3:** French Knot (1 strand) | | | |
| 862 | ● | 520 | Fern Green-dk. |

# General Instructions

**Fabrics:** Most designs in this book are worked on even-weave fabrics that are made especially for cross-stitch and can be found in your local needlework shop. If you cannot find a particular fabric, see Suppliers for ordering information. Fabrics used for models are identified in sample information by color, name, and thread count per inch.

**Preparing Fabric:** Cut fabric at least 3" larger on all sides than finished design size, or cut as indicated in sample information, to ensure enough space for matting, framing, and other finishing techniques for stitched piece. To keep fabric from fraying, whipstitch or machine-zigzag along all raw edges or apply liquid ravel preventer.

**Needles:** Choose a needle that will slip easily through fabric holes without piercing fabric threads. For fabric with 11 or fewer threads per inch, use needle size 24; for 14 threads per inch, use needle size 24 or 26; for 18 or more threads per inch, use needle size 26. Never leave needle in design area of fabric. It may leave rust or a permanent impression on fabric.

**Hoop or Frame:** Select a hoop or stretcher bar frame large enough to hold entire design. Using a hoop or frame keeps fabric taut and makes it easier to make uniform stitches. Place screw or clamp of hoop in a 10 o'clock position (or 2 o'clock, if you are left-handed) to keep it from catching floss.

**Centering Design:** To find center of *fabric*, fold it in half from top to bottom and then from left to right. The intersection of folds is center. To find center of *graph*, follow vertical and horizontal arrows until they intersect. Begin stitching center of graph at center of fabric.

**Floss:** Use 18" lengths of floss. For best coverage, separate strands. Dampen with wet sponge. Then put back together number of strands called for in color code.

**Securing Floss:** Bring needle and most of floss up through fabric, leaving a 1" tail of floss on underside. Secure floss tail with first few stitches.

Another method for securing floss is the waste knot. Knot floss and bring needle down through fabric about 1" from where first stitch will be taken. Plan placement of knot so that first 4 or 5 stitches cover and secure 1" of floss on back of fabric. After floss is secured, cut off knot.

To secure floss after stitching is completed, run needle under 4 or 5 stitches on back of design and clip ends close to fabric.

**Stitching Method:** For smooth stitches, use the push-and-pull method. Starting on wrong side of fabric, bring needle straight up, pulling floss completely through to right side. Reinsert needle and bring it back straight down, pulling needle and floss completely through to back of fabric. Keep floss flat but do not pull thread tight. For even stitches, tension should be consistent throughout.

**Carrying Floss:** To carry floss, weave it under previously worked stitches on back. Do not carry floss across any fabric that is not or will not be stitched. Loose strands, especially dark ones, will show through fabric.

**Cleaning Completed Work:** When stitching is complete, soak finished piece in cold water with mild soap for 5 to 10 minutes. Rinse thoroughly. Roll work in towel to remove excess water; do not wring. Place work face down on dry towel and, with iron on warm setting, press until work is dry.

**Beadwork:** First, bring needle up at lower left, slip bead on needle, and reinsert needle at upper right. Secure beads by stitching through beads again, from lower right to upper left (Diagram A). When working in rows, complete a row of diagonal half-cross stitches before returning to secure all beads.

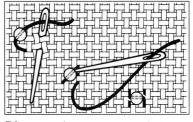

**Diagram A**

## Common Stitches

**Cross-stitch:** Make 1 cross-stitch for each symbol on chart. Bring needle up at A, down at B, up at C, and down again at D (Diagram B). For rows, stitch across fabric from left to right to make half-crosses and then back to complete stitches (Diagram C). All bottom half-crosses should slant in the same direction. All top half-crosses should slant in the opposite direction.

**Diagram B**

**Diagram C**

**Filet Cross-stitch:** Filet cross-stitch is simply cross-stitch that uses only 1 strand of embroidery floss. It is usually used for the background of a design, while the design itself is cross-stitched with enough strands to cover the fabric. When complete, the background resembles a delicate net.

**Three-quarter Stitch:** Three-quarter stitch is indicated on graph when a symbol fills only half of a square (Diagram D). If you are working over 1 thread, the short under-stitch will pierce the fabric thread; if you are working over 2 threads, it will pierce the hole between the 2 threads. In each case the long stitch is the overstitch, even though in some cases this may violate the rule that all stitches slant in the same direction.

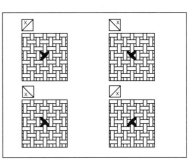

**Diagram D**

When 2 symbols occupy a single square on the graph, make a three-quarter stitch and a quarter stitch to fill the square. Which symbol takes which stitch will depend on the line you want to emphasize. Use three-quarter stitch to express dominant line or color (Diagram E).

**Diagram E**

**French Knot:** Bring needle up at A. Wrap floss around needle 2 times (unless indicated otherwise in instructions). Insert needle beside A, pulling floss until it fits snugly around needle. Pull needle through to back (Diagram F).

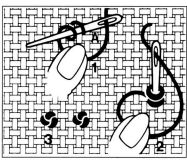

**Diagram F**

**Backstitch:** Complete all cross-stitches before working backstitches or other accent stitches. Working from right to left with 1 strand of floss (unless indicated

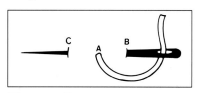

**Diagram G**

otherwise in color code), bring needle up at A, down at B, and up at C. Going back down at A, continue in this manner (Diagram G).

## Special Stitches

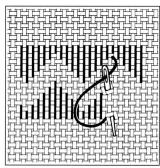

**Long Stitch**

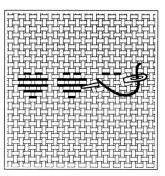

**Satin Stitch**

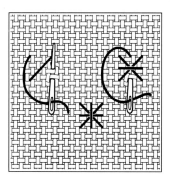

**Smyrna Cross-stitch**

*Suppliers*

**All products are available retail from Shepherd's Bush, 220 24th Street, Ogden UT 84401; (801) 399-4546; or for a merchant near you, write the following suppliers:**

**Zweigart Fabrics** — Zweigart/Joan Toggitt Ltd., Weston Canal Plaza, 2 Riverview Drive, Somerset, NJ 08873

**Zweigart Fabrics used:**
Cream Aida 11
Cream Aida 14
White Aida 14
White Aida 18
Beige Hardanger 22
Moss Green Lugana 25
White Dublin Linen 25
White Linda 27
Caramel Annabelle 28
Wedgwood Murano 30
White Murano 30
Cream Belfast Linen 32
Raw Belfast Linen 32
White Belfast Linen 32

**Vanessa-Ann Afghan Weave 18** — Chapelle Ltd., P.O. Box 9252, Newgate Station, Ogden, UT 84409

**Christmas Fingertip Towels (Deep Teal, Rich Cranberry) and Waste Canvas 10** — Charles Craft, P.O. Box 1049, Laurinburg, NC 28352

**Natural Dirty Linen 26** — Wichelt Imports, Inc., Rural Route 1, Stoddard, WI 54658

**Mill Hill Beads** — Mill Hill Division of Gay Bowles Sales, Inc., P.O. Box 1060, Janesville, WI 53547

**Balger Products** — Kreinik Mfg. Co., Inc., P.O. Box 1966, Parkersburg, WV 26102

**Overture Yarn** — Rainbow Gallery, 13756 Victory Boulevard, Van Nuys, CA 91401

**Broder Medicis Wool Yarn** — The DMC Corp., Port Kearney Building #10, South Kearney, NJ 07032-0650

**Small Candle Screen** — Sudberry House, P.O. Box 895, Old Lyme, CT 06371